HOUSE BOATS

LIVING ON THE WATER AROUND THE WORLD

MARK GABOR

Photographs by John Blaustein
with Eddy Posthuma de Boer
Pedar Ness
Mark Gabor

BALLANTINE BOOKS • NEW YORK

For my parents, Rose and Louis

Copyright © 1979 by Mark Gabor and Andreas Landshoff
Photographs copyright © 1979 by John Blaustein
Photographs copyright © 1979 by Eddy Posthuma de Boer
Photographs copyright © 1979 by Pedar Ness
Photographs copyright © 1979 by Mark Gabor

Library of Congress Cataloging in Publication Data

Gabor, Mark, 1939-
    Houseboats.

    1. House—boats. I. Landshoff, Andreas, joint author. II. Title.
GV836.G32   797.1′2   77-6136
ISBN 0-345-27312-5
ISBN 0-345-28117-9 ppbk

"A Mark Gabor/Andreas Landshoff Book"
Designed by Renée van de Griend

This edition published simultaneously in hardcover and trade paperback editions.
Manufactured in the United States of America

First Edition: February 1979

1 2 3 4 5 6 7 8 9 10

HOUSE BOATS

Other books by the author:

The Pin-up: A Modest History
Art of the Calendar
Vans and the Truckin' Life (Editor)

Contents

Introduction	6
Seattle	8
California	19
Florida	30
Louisiana	41
Hong Kong	48
Thailand	62
Kashmir	72
France	86
England	95
Holland	106
Turkey and Italy	126
Acknowledgments	128
Photography Credits	128

Introduction

Several hundred thousand people live on houseboats around the world. In some cultures the tradition is centuries old, in others it is a recent phenomenon. Houseboat living is an economic necessity in certain places. It may also be a family tradition. And again it may reflect a new and elite life-style in the midst of an affluent, land-based society. One common thread ties these social, economic, and historical conditions together: those living on houseboats—whether in America, Europe, or Asia—seem to love it. They are aware of a special feeling, a difference, a challenge, in spending their lives and raising their families on water.

There is something immediate about living on water. It is the constant motion of waves, currents, tides, and winds. A motion not so much observed as it is felt. One is not surrounded by it, but is part of it, *in* it. Because of the ever-changing character of water—whether it be the daily tides, flood conditions, drought, or seasonal weather changes—one's houseboat is always responding to its environment. And the houseboat dweller is continually aware of it. Communities of houseboats are exposed to the same external conditions, and the effect is to bring the people together, sharing the joys and challenges of living in such immediacy with the elements. In good weather the sun and water are just outside the door to be exploited for a wide range of recreational and leisure activities. In storms, floods, or extreme tides houseboat people work together to secure their dwellings safely to the moorings or to each other. The sense of community is pervasive.

Of course, there are many different kinds of houseboats around the globe. In Hong Kong and Thailand they are all working boats, used for fishing, transporting cargo, and vending along waterways. In Kashmir one finds, in addition to the working houseboats, two other types—residential, used by natives working in the city of Srinagar; and the famous "hotel houseboats," reserved for world travelers. In several countries in Europe, houseboats are primarily converted from retired river barges and small- to medium-sized cargo boats. In England one finds traditional narrow boats, Thames River barges, converted cargo sailboats, and "floating-homes," which may be simply defined as house-type structures built onto flat barge bases or pontoons. In America there are principally two kinds of houseboats. One is the retired or abandoned barge, tug, cargo, or fishing boat, either converted "as is" for living, or else using only its original hull as a base for a house-like superstructure. The other kind, by far the most popular in the country, is the floating home—which can range dramatically from a one-room shingled cabin on wooden pontoons, to a mobile-home-type squatter's shack supported by metal oil drums, to a three-story suburban palace on a reinforced ferro-concrete barge base.

What makes a houseboat a houseboat varies obviously from one culture to another. A working fishing boat in America is not a houseboat even though the crew may sleep on it. The reason is that crew members invariably have land houses as their principal dwellings. Yet in Hong Kong, a junk, the traditional working fishing boat, is a houseboat because it is the actual residence of the fisherman *and* his family. Thus, function is not necessarily a prime consideration in defining a houseboat. It may or may not be a working boat. The determining factor is whether it is the home of the individuals using it.

Another, more subtle, consideration is design, furnishings, and degree of conversion. Certain people live aboard sailboats and cabin cruisers. If these vessels are maintained with only their original appointments, are *conceptualized* by the owners as pleasure craft, and not modified to the extent of being "homey" (admittedly, a subjective assessment)—then one can only say that these are boats being lived on, not houseboats. Perhaps this notion can be understood better when seen in terms of utility. With the exception of working houseboats—that is, boats used equally as sources of income and principal residences—the main criterion for defining a houseboat is its primary usage. If it is mainly for travel, pleasure, or sport and is equipped accordingly, it cannot be correctly called a houseboat, even if people live on it during its usage. If, on the other hand, a boat is modified or converted appropriately for year-round living, and the people on it have established the vessel as their main or sole residence, then it is considered a houseboat.*

A houseboat does not necessarily have to be immobile. Obviously, it is essential for working houseboats to move. And often converted fishing boats, cargo boats, etc., which are moored as houseboats in one place for most of the time, are also used secondarily for vacations or touring. Other converted boats are too old or not mechanically fit to move, and thus are moored permanently. Finally, houseboats built specifically as floating homes are never moved (except for changing their moorings).

Perhaps the greatest problem facing houseboat dwellers in America and parts of Europe is the legality of houseboat living. For many years, houseboats held no legal status in terms of zoning laws, taxation, and building codes. Years ago houseboat owners needed only to find a moorage space—whether on a river bank, lakeside, canal, or in a bay—in order to go about the business of living on the water. These spaces were often free, though sometimes minimal moorage fees were paid to marinas or shoreside property owners. As years passed, local governments began to impose taxes on the houseboats, very often in return for little or no local services. The authorities often argued that houseboats are not properly maintained, and that the lack of adequate sewage and garbage disposal tends to create "ghettos on the waterfront." Private land developers, looking to build hotels, condominiums, resort marinas, etc., along shorelines, are known to pressure city

---

*In recent years a commercially made "houseboat" has gained great popularity in America and parts of Western Europe. It is essentially a cabin cruiser with square rooms built above the hull. It is intended exclusively for recreational purposes, and is rarely if ever used as a full-time living space. For these reasons, I have omitted this type of boat from the book.

elders to condemn individual houseboats and, more recently, entire communities of houseboats as unsanitary, substandard for living, water polluters, and even as "eyesores." For decades, these tensions have been a part of houseboat living in many areas of the Western world. Some houseboat communities have been abolished. Others have fought the establishment and won, but usually at substantial expense for the houseboat owners — personal property taxes, increased moorage fees, city or town taxes, and the cost of bringing a houseboat "up to code," meaning expensive plumbing, sewage systems, new electrical wiring, and so forth. The success of these houseboat owners has been dependent upon their ability to organize, usually in the form of houseboat associations, lobbying in numbers against the often unfair regulations imposed upon them.

It is not easy to organize people whose life-styles are so frequently tied to the concepts of individualism, free expression, and laissez-faire. Too often there is divisiveness within a given houseboat association. It seems apparent that those communities which hold together are the ones likely to succeed in securing their futures. Those which become factionalized seem doomed to fail.

If houseboat communities are not at their best when taking on the establishment, they are superbly united when sharing their skills, information, and resourcefulness at the moorage sites. Families care for each other's children. They often pool money and labor for repairs of their docks or each other's houseboats. They also share an esthetic — the experience of water living — to which nothing else can be quite compared. The serenity, the tranquility of calm days and nights. The drama of being tossed about by rough waters and strong winds. A constant sense of days and nights, of skies, and of seasons.

Houseboat people, by and large, are a hardy and independent group. They pride themselves on their ability to improvise, to respond to the often unpredictable demands of their natural environment. They gladly share their experiences, but vigorously defend the privacy of their space and time. The houseboat itself is an expression of that privacy, the individuality which often sets the water dweller apart from those living on terra firma.

On the pages that follow, one can see the widest variety of houseboats in the world. Whether one's personal taste leans toward handmade, rustic, one-room floatshacks, or long, narrow, traditional river barges, toward polished teak junks, or triumphs of architectural elegance — all these houseboats are expressions of the people who live on them, the people who can chant in unison: "Our boats are our homes!"

Seattle

Of all the houseboat areas in America, the Northwest is today the most stable, accepted, and traditional, with the longest history of houseboat living in the country. At present, there are nearly 450 legally zoned houseboats in the two main Seattle areas, Portage Bay and Lake Union.

In earlier years there were three bodies of water accommodating as many as 2,500 houseboats—Lake Union, Lake Washington, and the Duwamish River. It all started during the 1870's, when Puget Sound was bustling with maritime traffic and the waters were used extensively by the logging industry. Those involved with the waterways at that time were aided by various floating structures built on logs.* They were variously called floathouses, boathouses, and cookhouses, providing offices, bunks, and food for lumbermen and seamen alike.

The earliest residential houseboats in the Seattle area are recorded in the 1880's—lived on by mill workers and their families. This attracted the attention of more affluent families living in Seattle, who began to see the recreational possibilities of houseboats and thus built a number of elegant floating weekend cottages in and around the small residential colonies that were sprouting up on Lake Union in the 1890's. By the turn of the century Lake Union was popular with a variety of socio-economic groups. There were those who worked on the water or were in some way connected to the marine trade, and found it convenient and pleasant to live on houseboats. And there were others—the predecessors of most of today's American houseboaters—who simply loved the water and wanted to live closer to it.

Around 1900, Lake Washington became the fashionable place for houseboats—enormous ones, built by wealthy families, mainly for summer use. And increasingly the younger members of these families, especially the young marrieds, lived on the houseboats year round. These were the jet-setters of their day, and this was the thing to do. It made the society page.

The third area, the Duwamish River, was during the same period witnessing a houseboat growth similar to that of Lake Union: accommodating mill workers, seamen, and other working-class people.

In 1909, following the Alaskan gold rush, one of the first "world's fairs" was organized. It was the Alaska-Yukon-Pacific Exposition, celebrating the expansion of the Northwest. Visitors came to Seattle, the Expo headquarters, from all parts of the world to see "God's Country," to explore business ventures, and of course to have a jolly time. For this purpose dozens of "teahouses" were built on the Seattle waters—floating clubs, serving bootlegged liquor, entertainment, gambling, and some lively Western belles.

*The best wood for flotation is considered to be cedar, which gets waterlogged more slowly than spruce or fir. It is estimated that a four-foot-diameter cedar log takes 75 years to get waterlogged; spruce and fir, 25 years. All these logs are considered excellent means of flotation owing to their weight and density, which renders structures quite water-stable in most kinds of weather.

Following the Expo years (1909-10) many of the teahouses were converted for residential living—and some still exist. The oldest existing houseboat from that period and possibly the oldest in the U.S. was originally called "Hostess House." On land it was an information center for the Expo, and the place where people went to get hostesses, guides, and companions to show them around. It was put in the water in around 1910 and is still floating on Portage Bay.

By 1917, there were an estimated 2,500 houseboats in the Seattle area. But in that year, when Lake Washington was lowered eight feet to the level of the connecting bodies of water, most of the lake's houseboats were either abandoned or dismantled.

During the Depression years, houseboats boomed again for reasons different from those of earlier times. For the poor, houseboats offered the cheapest possible living, with the advantage of free food by means of fishing in the surrounding waters. Depression houseboat owners joined the Industrial Workers of the World, in which, as "Wobblies," they became part of a highly organized, anti-capitalist, pro-socialist movement for the rights of the poor. At the start of World War II there were approximately 2,000 houseboats in the Seattle area. As the war progressed, economic factors and the call to military duty caused a great many to disappear. The decline continued further, as a result of steady pressure through the years by Seattle's city elders, who wanted to collect taxes on houseboats. Also, the dwellings were considered undesirable. They were condemned as slums, particularly the clusters of poor squatters' boats in the Duwamish River. By the end of World War II, houseboats on this river were virtually eliminated by the city government. And on Lake Washington, the already dwindling numbers of owners chose to abandon their houseboats rather than fight city hall.

In 1952 an ordinance was passed declaring all houseboats unsanitary. Although there were several vain attempts by houseboat residents to contest the ruling and fight for rights to live in homes on the water, it wasn't until 1961-62 that a strong enough organization was formed, the Floating Home Association, to bargain effectively with the city elders. Soon new ordinances were passed, protecting the houseboats. And in 1963 a program was implemented whereby all existing houseboats—540 at the time—agreed to cooperate in the installation of all necessary plumbing to connect directly with the city's sewage system. The task took five years, during which time approximately 100 houseboats were lost because they were obsolete, unable to be plumbed—leaving a total of 444 legal houseboats in Seattle. Today, most are still floating. Some have been replaced by new and modern floating homes. But the 444 moorage spaces are secure, whether the houseboats are old or new.

Sewage was the key to the legal problem in Seattle. It may be interesting to observe the plight of other houseboat communities in the U.S. and abroad, threatened in some way by the authorities—in places like Miami Beach, Sausalito, Paris, London, and Amsterdam. But Seattle has solved its problem. Not only are the houseboats legally acceptable, but they are gaining status all the time.

The moorings are treated as land lots, and the houseboats as bona fide houses. Real estate taxes are paid through moorage fees. And personal property taxes are levied on the basis of single-family dwellings. The houseboats are today considered by many to be historical landmarks.

Many of the houseboats on Portage Bay and Lake Union are architectural gems, and a few are considered masterpieces. Most, however, are best described as middle-sized, imaginative, and charming floating homes, varying from shaped Plexiglas designs to handmade, rustic wood motifs. Others, still, look like ordinary modest cabins on the water. Each seems to have a different personality, but all somehow fit together in mixed communities that have many interests and problems in common — particularly those having to do directly with houseboat living.

The residents of Seattle's water homes all appear to enjoy the life-style. They seem unanimous in their love of the water — sailing, swimming, fishing, and the constant motion of waves, currents, and tides. It is a tranquil feeling — quite apart and different from living on land. Some of the differences are obvious, some subtle. One Seattle houseboater put it this way: "I'm a water freak. I don't like land things. You might not understand this, but I see a big difference between mowing a lawn or pulling weeds as compared to tending the potted plants on my boat. When I want it — which isn't very often — I can always have the city. We're very close to the city. But this kind of life gets to you — you really prefer to hang out at home. In fact my houseboat is a perpetual vacation."

Other Seattle houseboat dwellers stress the feeling of community, a certain finiteness of their moored environment, usually occupying a limited space along the waterfront, with neighbors close by, friendlier than most land people, and more prone to sharing their time, skills, and ideas.

North of Seattle is a small town* near the Skagit River inhabited by a growing colony of artists, writers, carpenters, and craftspeople. Some live in the town, some in the woods, some on the river, and others in surrounding estuaries.

*In a cordial exchange of information, residents asked that the town "remain anonymous" in this book for reasons of privacy.

There is a small old marina under a bright red-orange modern bridge, with perhaps a dozen quite varied houseboats mixed in with tugs, dredges, and fishing boats. One houseboat is a tractor trailer set into a flat barge base, another a small rectangular cottage snugged into a 25-foot open dory. Most seem thrown together resourcefully, from whatever found structures were apparently available in the general area. But one houseboat stands out as a work of art in itself. It's a beautiful, brown-shingled, handmade floating fairy-tale house, complete with stovepipe chimney and stained-glass windows.

Some artists living nearby gave their reasons for living at this quaint marina. "We like the nature aspect of the river. The currents, fish, kelp, and ducks all get under your skin after a while." One person likes the area because "There are lotsa other artists here." Another thinks she is going to be a writer. And still another, a sculptor, has been "passing through for several months," on his way to Alaska to make some money fishing.

Not far from this marina is an estuary of the river, a place where the tides are fairly extreme so that the highs fill the area with water while the lows leave it a vast mudhole. Over a narrow wooden boardwalk leading out to a dense few acres of reeds there are four small houses called "floatshacks." Most of the time they sit on the mud, but with the high tide they float completely on the moss-covered logs supporting them. The boardwalk floats with the tide, too, as does the dock at the end of the reeds.

The floatshacks are of pure rustic materials and designs. They seem reminiscent of early settlers' cabins. The roofs are covered with yellow-green moss, and various driftwood art-constructions adorn the decks around the houses.

Floatshacks are an unusual, if not unique, form of houseboat. They were not originated by the artists now living in them. They were built during the Depression by poor fishermen, who, with their families, lived "away from it all" and fed themselves almost entirely from the great runs of salmon on the Skagit River. (The fish were cured and dried so that they could be eaten through an entire winter.)

The floatshacks were abandoned after the Depression and most were destroyed by the elements. A few structures remained through the years. It is these that local artists have reconstructed into their present, pristine form.

Group of modern, beautifully designed
houseboats in a floating moorage at Portage Bay,
in the Seattle, Washington, area.

A

A and.*B:* two views of houseboat "11" at the same dock as previous group. The elegant all-wood exterior is set off by tastefully placed potted plants.

C: interior view of dining area in Portage Bay houseboat, with large stained-glass window behind tree plant. The view outside shows clearly the closeness and immediate access to the water.

C

B

Multi-storied houseboat on Portage Bay, with ample dock space by the sun deck for visiting boats.

On a moody afternoon at Portage Bay, several interesting contrasts can be seen — a modern glass-and-Plexiglas houseboat and behind it the larger, brown wooden floating home two stories high. In the background, houses line the hills around Portage Bay in this suburban area of Seattle.

Exterior and interior views of a handcrafted houseboat on Lake Union, in the Seattle area. The original structure was built in the 1950s; the present owner has redone the boat since he took it over in 1974. The interior has an open sleeping deck above the front doors, with windows looking out onto the lake and two skylights that open and close directly over the bed. Behind the front sitting room are a full kitchen and dining area; to the side, a children's bedroom.

Two characteristic luxury floating homes on Lake Union. Here large glass windows are used to get the best view of the sprawling lake and take advantage of the dramatic skies so often seen in this area.

This splendid floating home was planned and built by the present owner with architect J. W. P. Olson. Completed about 1975, the houseboat was designed with the idea of "taking in the beautiful views all around" through the use of large corner windows reaching up to the second story of the boat and curving overhead as skylights. Most of the main downstairs area is open to the full height of the houseboat, creating a luxurious spaciousness throughout. A balcony runs along much of the second story, providing access to bedrooms and other smaller rooms. The houseboat occupies a corner space in its Lake Union moorage, thus substantially increasing the view of its surroundings.

Exterior and interior views of a traditional Seattle houseboat, built in 1926 and expanded in 1948. The present owner, who has had it since 1968, has completely redesigned the outside and inside of this richly textured water dwelling. Plants are found throughout, as well as hanging, sun-reflecting crystals and an array of colorful artifacts. With the contrasting high-rise apartments behind, this houseboat is a visual treat among the Lake Union population.

Exterior and detail from a unique handmade houseboat cozily moored alongside a tugboat on the Skagit River, near a small town in Washington. This charming wood-shingled houseboat reflects the originality of design and style so often seen in handmade houseboats. Charmingly shaped windows and doors are echoed in the interior by small, quaint, and variously shaped rooms, with lovely furniture, hangings, and artworks.

In the Skagit region, a "floatshack" hides in the tall reeds surrounding an estuary. Built on logs, this rural water dwelling floats when the tide comes in, and sits on mud the rest of the time. Note the colorful moss-covered roof and sculpture garden of found objects on the floatshack's deck.

California

Nowhere are houseboats so well known in the U.S. as in California, particularly in the San Francisco Bay area. California houseboating goes as far back as the 1880's, when a colony of "arks" existed in Belvedere. The arks were generally large and rectangular, with a deck all around and a porch (covered or open) at one end. They were the earliest form of floating homes, used chiefly as warm-weather recreational boats in various quiet waterways, then pulled ashore during the winter in Belvedere Lagoon, near Corinthian Island. The original ark community was monied. Fresh food was sold to the ark dwellers from a steady stream of small rowboats tending the larger houseboats. And small steamers provided services to and from the shore — taxiing residents and guests, delivering drinking water and other supplies.

In 1906 an earthquake destroyed many homes, businesses, and personal fortunes in San Francisco, forcing many ark owners to live on their boats all year round. But in later decades, the worsening economic conditions of the Depression and two World Wars gradually saw the decline of the Belvedere arks. Only a few exist today. They are in Tiburon, California, converted to boutiques on "Ark Row."

Along Corte Madera Creek, from north of Larkspur south to Greenbrae, the 1890's saw another early California ark colony. Originally inhabited by seamen, fishermen, and duck hunters, the colony was expanded through the years by the addition of summer and weekend residents. The community was virtually undisturbed through the early decades of the century. Some of the arks were pulled up on the marshes and became shoreside land houses. Others were built up on pilings. Many of those that were originally intended for summer use were converted to year-round dwellings.

In the 1960's several factors combined to threaten and finally eliminate the Corte Madera Creek community. Private land developers began buying up the property from the State Lands Commission, resulting in a rash of evictions affecting most of the arks resting on the land. As for the floating arks, owing to gradual seepage into the creek's bed (of silt, gold-mining waste, and earth washed away from construction sites in the Marin County hills), the Army Engineering Corps was instructed to dredge the creek using a procedure that forced most of the arks forever from the area. In 1967 the houseboat community on Corte Madera Creek came to an end.

Other houseboat colonies in the Bay area have met with the same or similar fates in the 1970's. And today only a handful of legal houseboat communities thrive in the San Francisco area — at the Barnhill Marina in the Alameda Estuary, the Berkeley Marina, the Point San Pablo Yacht Harbor in the Richmond area, Mill Valley, and a few other places.

The Barnhill Marina is exclusively for houseboats. They are the typical middle-class floating-home variety, ranging in value from $25,000 to $50,000. Moorage (not including utilities) fees range from about $135 to $150 per month. Each houseboat is fully sewered and floats on concrete or fiberglass pontoons or full barge bases. The marina was built around 1962 and consists of floating docks equipped to supply water and electricity. Barnhill is legal for houseboat living, as it conforms to all the necessary building codes.

The huge Berkeley Marina, at the foot of the Berkeley hills, contains mostly sailboats and cabin cruisers, but has a few comfortable-looking houseboats scattered here and there on its many docks.

The Point San Pablo Yacht Harbor is a smallish marina on San Pablo Bay, opposite Petaluma, California, and near Point Pinole (to the east). The marina is considered "out-of-the-way," a rural place for people who cherish their privacy and the chance to do their own thing, quietly. It has about ten houseboats, a few of which are handmade and of special interest. One of them has a charming steeple at one end, so that the boat when viewed from a certain angle resembles a traditional small-town church (p.28). Another is designed around the form of a figure eight. Built on a ferro-concrete barge-type base, it has a sundeck on the top level leading into the master bedroom, which is only about four feet high. The large, open, split-level kitchen/dining/living area is the core of the houseboat. Additional bedrooms (childrens'), bathroom, playroom, and storage compartments are reached through trapdoors leading from the living area through a maze of four-foot-high passageways which can be traveled only on hands and knees. The effect of this original design is that of a playhouse for adults and children alike. The owners (he's a carpenter, she's a pianist) enjoy living on the water. They like the feeling of motion and very much enjoy their new hobby of kayaking all around the bay. They don't contemplate living on land again.

The largest, most famous, and now most controversial houseboat area in California is in Sausalito. There one finds a series of docks containing hundreds of houseboats of every size, shape, and description. Each dock, referred to as a "gate" in Sausalito, has its own distinct personality. Houseboats range from the expensive, elegant, floating-home type, to medium-sized handcrafted boats that look like floating sculpture, and to unique water-shanties simply thrown together, such as the VW microbus sitting in the middle of a small open dinghy (p.22). Nowhere else is there such a concentration of different, if not disparate, houseboats as in Sausalito.

The rise in houseboat living came to this town following World War II. At that time Sausalito began attracting many writers, painters, and craftspeople, whose creativity was applied to the challenge of living cheaply on water. The artists did not confine themselves to a particular type of houseboat construction. They used whatever resources were available, including abandoned ferries and military hulls, scraps of metal and wood gathered inland, and flotsam and jetsam. Ignoring building codes and most rules and regulations, the artists wound up creating an impressive conglomeration of live-in sculpture — patched, fantasy structures, vividly colored in an endless variety of paints and other materials. Most have no electricity, phones, or running water. These houseboats reside at several docks, known collectively as Waldo Point.

Through recent decades Waldo Point has been a haven for the poor artist, with moorage fees as low as $25 per month for a small houseboat. To the inexperienced eye, the maze of docks and gangplanks, the random positioning of the 203 houseboats, and the accumulation of apparent junk lying about lead one to believe it is an area characterized by squalor and chaos. But that is far from the truth. Each dock is its own neighborhood, with names like "Muck and Mire Boulevard" and "Sleazie's." Everyone knows where everyone else lives. The positioning of the boats is not so much random as it is complex, differing at each bend and turn along the dockways as an expression of the artists' desires to be unregimented, improvisational. The so-called junk lying about is a colossal stockpile of building and sculptural materials — essentially an effort to recycle what middle-class society would casually discard as obsolete.

Waldo Point may soon face its toughest test for survival if the new owners of the property go through with plans to bring all the houseboats "up to code," to construct new, straight docks, and to make legal sewerage a requirement. (At present most Waldo Point inhabitants are proud of their method of handling human waste. They use compost privies, or "pooperators," which are large, vented drums with toilet seats on top, containing layers of wood chips. After each usage sawdust is added. When the drum is full, it is sealed and stored for six months during which time the contents decompose. After pasturization, the mixture can be bagged and sold as fertilizer or at the very least as landfill. When one thinks of the amount of flush water saved by not using conventional toilets, the compost privy must be considered a first-rate ecological device.)

The Waldo Point inhabitants are being pressured nevertheless. Perhaps it is their free-and-easy life-style that irritates the property developers. It is more likely a matter of economics. More money in the form of higher moorage fees can be made if the docks are improved and the houseboats plumbed, wired, and plugged into a conventional sewage system. Neighboring docks have conformed to the new requirements. There is a certain enmity — snobbism versus anti-snobbism — along the docks in Sausalito. Worse still, there is divisiveness within the two main gates comprising Waldo Point. The ultimate danger is that poorer artists will lose the right to be, and remain, poor. They regard the situation as a moral struggle against a society in which order and respectability are more important than personal freedom, and profits are more desirable than simple ecology.

Many people outside Waldo Point are concerned with this symbolic struggle. The most impressive statement of support has come from Buckminster Fuller: "America has many groups of youths realistically living their attempt to rectify inequities outstanding in American life . . . The Waldo Point group in Sausalito, California, establish their floating community on old boats, barges, floating homes, or shacks as a water colony. They have undertaken to educate their children in the simplicity of a century-ago pioneer America. After a score of successful years of self-organization they are now threatened with expulsion from their waterfront to make way for a rich middle-class houseboat marina. We hope that America will catch on quickly enough to save them" (from a telegram published in Waldo Point's *Garlic Press*, Vol. III, No. 1, March 1977).

Next to the Sausalito houseboat colony, but technically in Mill Valley, California, are several docks containing some fairly elegant floating homes, some owned by people who are concerned with the "messiness" of their Waldo Point neighbors. The docks are lined with houseboats in the $25,000-and-up price range. And the moorage fees are in the $400-$500 per month range. The residents have a variety of vocations — there are business people, a flying instructor, music arranger, professional musician.

One owner, a produce broker, lives in an attractive redwood houseboat, with skylights and shaped windows. It was designed by an architect and built by two carpenters over a period of one and a half years. The ceilings are made of pine and the closets are all cedar. The 20×40 foot floating home has a large spiral staircase leading from the full-sized downstairs living room with a round chrome fireplace and a large Japanese-style bath, to the upstairs floor which has the kitchen, dining area, sitting room, and bedroom. The houseboat also has a comfortable sun deck. Completed in 1974, it is now valued at around $75,000.

Although the houseboats and the residents at Mill Valley serve as a contrast to their neighbors at Waldo Point, certain apparently universal houseboat values are shared by all — the abiding love of the water, an attraction to the ever-changing scenery, and the sense of cooperation and community, especially within one's own dock area.

Alongside the door of one of Waldo Point's "gates" (docks), a converted motor launch with a flat-roofed space built above the stern and a pointed wood-shingled superstructure ending at the bow.

One of several retired ferries at Waldo Point, this hulk houses a number of water dwellers in somewhat rundown quarters. The ferry dwarfs a mini-houseboat to the right.

A

B

A selection of small, handmade, improvised Waldo Point houseboats, showing the variety and creative use of materials so characteristic of this controversial community. *A:* a recycled VW microbus serves as the living structure on this open life-saving boat. *B:* a fairyland façade, with teardrop windows, adorns the bow of this retired, metal-hulled boat. *C:* an old mobile home supported by pontoon-like logs serves as another recycled dwelling for a Sausalito resident. *D:* a potpourri of found materials serves as structure and design for this small house, set upon an open-hulled boat.

C

D

The well-known and often photographed mailboxes for residents of Waldo Point.

Interior of Sausalito houseboat, showing informal and efficient use of space, with sleeping deck above. The boat measures 28 × 16 feet.

A row of fanciful and original houseboats with a
distinct California flair line a dock not far from
Waldo Point. Most of the houseboats in this
general area rest on mud for an average of a few
hours a day when the tide is out.

This elegant Sausalito houseboat has an antique
quality in its exterior, and almost appears to be
moored to its own decks and supporting beams.

◀
Aerial view of some of the more expensive, often
elegant floating homes in the Sausalito area. The
straight, fairly modern docks are in contrast to the
winding walkways at Waldo Point.

Exterior and interior detail of a custom-built houseboat in Mill Valley, California, adjacent to the Sausalito houseboat sites. This splendidly appointed floating home is made of redwood, with pine ceilings and cedar closets. A two-story structure, the upper level contains kitchen, sitting room, and open bedroom area. Below is a large living area with a chrome fireplace and Japanese-style bath. A wide spiral staircase connects the two levels. The 20 × 40 foot houseboat, designed by an architect, took one and one half years to build and was completed in 1974. The present owner and his family have a great love of the water. Living on a houseboat affords them beautiful and changing scenic views, a closeness with waterfowl, a sense of peace and quiet.

Interior view of skylighted sleeping loft on a 25 ×
15 foot houseboat in Sausalito. The dwelling, built
in 1969, has since 1973 been the home of its
present owner, who regards houseboat living as
"being perpetually on vacation." Below the loft is
the open living room with a hooded fireplace, a
full kitchen, and a counter dividing the space.
Above the sleeping loft there is a sun deck.

A super-elegant floating home in Sausalito looks
as if it really *is* on the lawn of a rich U.S. suburb.

Left: This highly original design, with its church-like façade, is moored at a small, relatively isolated marina at Point Richmond, California.

At the same marina, two interior views of a 16 × 32 foot houseboat built by a carpenter. He, his wife (a musician), and their two lively children find it ideal for their needs. The main deck is a split-level, with dining area and living room (including piano) raised and kitchen a few steps lower, *B*, near the porched entrance. At the top of the houseboat is a low-ceilinged circular loft bedroom, *A*, leading onto a sun deck and below the main level are children's bedrooms, a bathroom, play areas, and several storage bins.

A

B

Florida

The State of Florida is in the midst of a "boom" period. There is rampant construction of hotels, motels, condominiums, sprawling shopping centers. In addition, one finds ever-increasing numbers of restaurants, country clubs, golf courses, discotheques, and other amusement and recreational facilities. Many of the permanent residents are involved in this growth process — from construction workers to entrepreneurs, from bartenders to yacht builders. The working population of Florida caters by and large to the rich and to the retired; they consider themselves more "native" to the state, closer to the land and water, than those people who have moved there to enjoy their retirement years in a semi-tropical climate.

A certain number of the working population take pride in living on houseboats, most often called "floating homes" in this part of the United States. Florida's houseboats are not all bunched together or localized in one main area, and architecturally are of many styles. They represent a wide swath of socio-economic living — from handmade, artistic communal dwellings starting at several hundred dollars each, to huge, architect-designed, three-deck, $200,000 ultra-luxury floating mansions. The handmade variety are generally small, gutted, primitive floating structures no bigger than camping trailers, while the expensive, fancier boats have every conceivable modern gadget found on land houses — quadraphonic sound wired throughout, indirect lighting, water beds, color televisions, dishwashers, air conditioning, wall-to-wall carpeting, swinging seats, awninged sun roofs, saunas, etc.

Some of the grander of Florida's floating homes are found on Indian Creek, which might be more familiar to the reader as the narrow canal running alongside Miami Beach's famous Collins Avenue, where some of Florida's most sumptuous high-rise hotels stand. Right in the exclusive middle of Miami Beach, dwarfed by these huge structures, are dozens of handsome middle- and upper-middle-class houseboats, ranging in size from 20 × 30 feet to 40 × 65 feet and in value from $25,000 to $150,000 — all air-conditioned. Even the smaller-sized water dwellings on Indian Creek are beautifully designed inside and out, neatly painted, and well appointed (pp.36–37). Each houseboat has its own personality and style — sloping architecture with a maze of angular shapes; outdoor decks overflowing with green potted plants and flowers; textured surfaces of shimmering fiberglass; or a sinister black-smoked glass, low-floating houseboat eerily reminiscent of the Confederate warship *Merrimac*.

Indian Creek houseboats are under close scrutiny by the Miami Beach city authorities. Some irascible landlubbers have become over-zealous ecologists, offended by the notion that human waste (whether or not pre-treated in organic chemical tanks) is released into the water rather than piped into the city's sewage system. The officials are not aware of how negligible is the pollution caused by human waste, compared to the non-biodegradable industrial wastes dumped daily into the Florida waterways only a few miles away. The authorities frown on houseboat living in Miami Beach, but no serious confrontation has occurred. Perhaps it's understood that the houseboat community lends charm and individualism to the towering impersonality of the "million dollar mile" of huge resort hotels.

Indian Creek houseboats get their electricity from power jacks (much like those at standard marinas) built onto the moorings where they tie up. Water is usually run onto the houseboat through hoses attached to taps, also situated at the edge of the mooring. Sometimes, however, water is hand-carried to the houseboat and stored in raised tanks, so that it flows by gravitation.

Up the Miami River, northwest toward the Everglades, is a mariner's paradise — large commercial foreign and domestic cargo ships, oceangoing cabin cruisers, 110-foot yachts and 12-foot sailboats, tugboats, tenders, outboards of all sizes and shapes. And, of course, houseboats. Not as well scrubbed as those on Indian Creek, but some just as large, and others no bigger than a camping van. Altogether a little scruffier than their cousins on Indian Creek, but also more anonymous, more private, and more spread out along the riverside (p.32). Most have small or medium-sized motorboats tied up alongside, a sign that the inhabitants enjoy other parts of the river and connecting bodies of water.

There is an unusual marina on Harbor Island, by a causeway in the middle of Biscayne Bay. The marina is called Harbour West Yacht Club, but it has virtually no yachts, just houseboats — and a few are unique. There's a pseudo-Oriental boat, 30 × 60 feet, painted red and black with a Chinese dragon on one side and a single room on the top deck. The interior decor has to be called "Asian funk," so heavily influenced is it by the Western conception of the Orient. Another conspicuously elegant houseboat, out at the end of the pier, estimated to be in the $125,000 price range, is the kind one would expect to see on Indian Creek. But here it is on Harbor Island, rarely used by its owner. It's a visual delight, a multi-layered, low-roofed, double-hooded dwelling, with skylights on top (p.39). The other houseboats at the marina are middle-sized, rather conventional "shoe boxes" — a term used to describe what might be an ordinary suburban house simply transposed to a barge base, sitting on water instead of a lawn. Harbour West is mostly a family community, people that are working the nine-to-five week and enjoying the special experience of houseboat living in the evenings and on weekends the year round.

In North Miami there are several interesting marinas next to each other. At Maule Lake Marina, one finds a pleasant mix of cabin cruisers, yachts, and houseboats. The houseboats are varied, but not outstanding, most being fairly modern, boxy, and not particularly harmonious with the nautical surroundings. But one place stands out — truly a "floating home." For, as it turns out, this lovely adobe-colored, two-story dwelling was never meant to be a houseboat (p.40). It was originally built in 1971–72 in Chile by a contractor hoping to use it as a prototype for a large building complex in Florida. The house was put on a barge and towed to Florida, where it was examined by the Buildings Department and rejected for technical reasons. Rather than tow it south again, the house was left on the barge and moored at a marina. In 1973 the present owners purchased the house, and, rejecting the idea of moving the house onto land, moved straight into their "floating home."

Next to Maule Lake is Snug Harbor Marina, smaller and poorer than its neighbor. Snug Harbor instantly has the feel of a community. It is dominated by a resourceful group of young individuals — carpenters, technicians, craftspeople, schoolteachers, artists, and jewelry makers and dealers. They are people with many different vocations, but they share one common interest, and that is the houseboat. They make all their own fixtures and accoutrements — "shaping the space, and digging on nature." One handsome young houseboater is a rather serious-minded pizza chef, whose idea of a fulfilling vacation is traveling around the United States on his motorcycle, stopping at almost every pizza parlor along the way and sampling the different styles and tastes of this popular dish.

The Snug Harbor boats are quite small, and moored very close to one another. Yet they do not appear overcrowded at the marina, for one houseboat seems almost a part of the next. There is a steady flow of rock music spilling out of odd-shaped windows and beaded doorways; sporadic sounds of hammers and drills; a clear smell of incense; and dozens of cats and dogs lying about the moorage. Tools and skills are shared at Snug Harbor. Food and wine on occasion. But privacy is maintained — each person has his or her own life to lead. And in that context a charming and friendly community thrives (p.33).

Less than an hour's drive from Miami Beach is Fort Lauderdale, another of Florida's renowned playgrounds. Miles of clean white beach and clear ocean water — most popular with the college set. Just a few miles inland from the coast is a remarkable floating facility, Marina Bay (p.34). On an expanded section of New River (widened in the late sixties as a result of dredging for landfill to build nearby Interstate Highway 95) is a large group of modern two-story houseboats, collectively called a "floating hotel." There are about 30 boats in all, each with four air-conditioned rentable units (60 rooms, 75 suites). Adjacent to the houseboats is a modern boat marina, where large yachts also dock. The yachtsmen and hotel guests alike enjoy Marina Bay's many recreational features — twelve tennis courts, saunas, swimming pool, clubhouse, bar, and a top-rated restaurant that earns Marina Bay over $3.5 million annually. Marina Bay is also a private club serving permanent residents of Fort Lauderdale and vicinity. Only club members (over 6,000 and growing) and hotel and marina guests can use the restaurant and facilities.

The Marina Bay property (i.e., the area where the land was dredged) was purchased in 1971 for approximately $1.5 million and is now valued at over $5 million. All the docks are floating, which means that docks, houseboats, and yachts all rise and fall with the tide, and the level between docks and boats never changes, unlike most conventional marinas. Marina Bay is completely sewered, treating all its waste in a chemical tank, then disposing of it through a standard sewer system. As a result of this, and attention to standard building codes, Marina Bay is the only legally zoned houseboat area in Florida.

Opposite the long, "hotel"-lined docks of Marina Bay are two extraordinary residential houseboats, approximately 50×30 feet. One of them, costing $90,000 to build and $60,000 to furnish, may be described as a two-family structure — one half occupied by the president of Marina Bay, the other half by a doctor. It is in the luxury houseboat class — two stories, large rooms, fully carpeted floors, marbled bathrooms, air conditioning, and splendid furnishings. Next to it is the second luxury dwelling. It is the same size, but is not divided for two families. Owned by a successful executive from the Midwest, it is even more elaborate than its neighbor. The roof is used as a sun deck, shaded by an attractive yellow-and-white awning. The houseboat has several guest bedrooms and a huge master bedroom with one wall completely mirrored. The main living room, on the lower level, sprawls with modern furniture, sculpture, and track lighting. The center table has its own built-in lighting system. Stereo sound runs throughout the interior, and a floor-to-ceiling panel behind the bar opens up to reveal a fully equipped kitchen. This houseboat cost an estimated $100,000 to build and another $100,000 to furnish. It is a floating palace — possibly the most lavish and luxurious houseboat in existence.

Florida's houseboats exhibit a tremendous range of life-styles, but here, too, all the inhabitants share a love of the water; a sense of being different from and freer than the average land dweller; a closeness to their natural surroundings; and always the sensation of motion, the gentle rocking on water.

Left: these large, comfortable floating homes rest in the quiet waters of the Miami River. As one can see, the smaller boats tied alongside are evidence that recreational boating in the Miami waterways is part of houseboat living there.

Right: at the Snug Harbor Marina, in North Miami Beach, small, inexpensive houseboats are built or restored by young people living in a communal atmosphere. *A:* a friend helps his neighbor install a window panel. *B:* an attractive young woman waves a friendly greeting while listening to rock music in the doorway of a characteristic Snug Harbor houseboat.

A

B

A

B

C

Left and right: Marina Bay at Fort Lauderdale, Florida—a multimillion-dollar complex of floating hotels, moored on modern concrete floating docks. *A:* two characteristic rows of rentable, motel-like suites, behind them the antique tin roof covering the clubhouse and highly rated restaurant. *B:* the "back porches" of two of the most expensive and luxurious private floating homes in the country. *C:* the sun-deck roof, with bar, on one of the two previous houseboats. *D:* mirrored, tastefully furnished bedroom beneath the sun deck. *E:* living room of the same house-boat, showing custom-designed coffee table with its own interior lighting. *F:* lavishly designed bathroom on one of the private luxury floating homes.

D

F

E

Medium-sized houseboat on Indian Creek, running alongside Miami Beach's famous hotel-filled Collins Avenue. The exterior has an elongated shingled, hood-like roof, shrouding a double window that looks out onto the waterway. The main room of the interior uses the full height of the structure to give a feeling of spaciousness. Next to this room are the kitchen and bath area, over which is the sleeping loft (from which this photo was taken).

A

Two sumptuous floating homes on Indian Creek.
A: modern split-level, as seen from the water,
with new high-rise luxury building in backdrop.
B: textured fiberglass, box-type houseboat as seen
from its moorage dock.

B

At the Harbour West Yacht Club in Biscayne Bay, Miami Beach, is this U.S.-built houseboat designed with an Oriental motif. Measuring 60 × 30 feet, the red-and-black floating home was built in the mid-sixties. It rests on fiberglass-covered plywood pontoons, and has two levels — on top, a sun deck surrounding a small bedroom, and, below, the living room, dining area, kitchen, two bathrooms, and master bedroom with a waterbed. *A:* the full exterior. *B:* the Orientalized front door. *C:* At the end of one of the docks in the same marina is this impressive multi-leveled floating home.

A

B

C

At Maule Lake Marina north of Miami is a rather special houseboat, special in that it was built in Chile as a prototype for a series of prefabricated land houses, but did not pass inspection by the Florida authorities. Towed north on a barge, it was left as a "house on a barge" until the present owners took it over as their floating home, furnishing it and filling it inside and out with colorful and rare plants. *A:* some of the stunning plants in front of the outdoor spiral staircase leading to the upper level. *B:* an office/study with hand-carved bookcases.

B

A

Louisiana

The quest for different and unusual types of houseboats led to Louisiana, particularly to the bayou country. Central New Orleans has no houseboats within the city limits. North of the city is huge Lake Pontchartrain, and there, on the south shore, two large marinas are situated. At the New Orleans Marina there are a few undistinguished houseboats amid several hundred sailboats. The same applies to the adjacent and more exclusive Southern Yacht Club. There is, however, one charming houseboat whose decor is reminiscent of a Mississippi riverboat. Nearby the two marinas is West End Park, where several large-sized, luxury-type floating homes are tied up along one pier.

One of the houseboats is owned by a juvenile-probation officer who swears by houseboat living. He can't stand concrete jungles, and enjoys "having everything here — sailboat, car, view, water, and freedom to move." Anytime he decides he's unhappy with his present location, he can simply tow his houseboat to another mooring. The 20 × 45 foot floating home was designed and built by the owner in 1971. He constructed a special barge-type base, compartmentalized into 20 sections, each watertight and independent from the others. He calculated that it would take only three of these compartments to support the weight of the boat and thus feels quite safe in case the base springs a few leaks. He also devised his own ventilation system for the base to keep the inside walls dry and free of rot. On his upper floor, reached by a spiral staircase, is a huge bedroom about three-fourths the size of the houseboat, with glass doors leading to a comfortable sun deck. The bed is suspended from the ceiling by a crisscross of cables, about one-eighth inch thick. The cable arrangement, though hardly visible, holds the bed completely steady — it seems almost like a magic trick. There are also a large closet area and a bathroom with a handmade, oversized tub (or an undersized pool?) — very nice for sipping wine by candlelight with special guests. Downstairs is the large living room and bar, well stocked with wine by the case. The boat, which cost an estimated $85,000, has a hooded fireplace, an unusual feature in a Southern houseboat, but welcome in New Orleans where it can be cold and damp in winter.

The neighboring houseboat is built on the same size and style barge base. The owner, a young and prosperous businessman, designed and started building his house in 1973. He explained that the houseboat was top-heavy, owing to the lightweight construction of the hull (like his neighbor's, it is wood, covered and sealed with fiberglass). He believes the ideal base should be made of ferro-concrete, which has the necessary weight and a much longer life than fiberglass-on-wood. There are several outstanding features of this modern houseboat, valued at approximately $85,000. Downstairs the resourceful owner built into a wall a colossal stereo outfit, a bi-amp system, with enough sound capacity to fill several stadiums. The tall speakers, situated in two corners of the living room, were custom-made for the other sound components. Another unique feature of the houseboat is a dark blue, shaped bathtub large enough for two, entirely designed and molded by the owner. The master bed is king-size and built into a handmade frame that is fully carpeted in blue shag. At the head of the bed is a mirrored wall. The bedroom is softly lit with modern stainless-steel light fixtures.

The Pearl River is the eastern border between Louisiana and Mississippi. Running parallel is a much narrower tributary, the West Pearl River. And from this muddy waterway many bayous split off. In the vicinity of the town of Pearl River, near the junction of Interstate Highways 10 and 59, is a group of typical bayou houseboats. They are poor indeed, some resembling the mobile homes seen in trailer parks throughout rural America, but here floating in the serene beauty of a Louisiana bayou. Others look simply like land shacks set on barrels, pontoons, or barge bases in the water. Their seemingly tranquil setting is abruptly if elegantly interrupted by the huge Interstate Highway overpass. It is altogether an environment of incongruity — especially when one adds to it the intermittent roar of 18-wheeler trucks flying across the overpass at 70 miles per hour.

Cruising around this bayou in a small boat, one can see other houseboats out of view from the land. Some of them are used on weekends only, but many of the dozen or so in this bayou are lived on full-time by individuals and families. Most of the people live here because they are poor — and in the bayou there are no rents to pay and no taxes on the houseboats or the water on which they unobtrusively rest. Metered electricity is available from nearby power poles; gas comes from propane tanks delivered to the water's edge; and water is carried onto the houseboats in plastic jugs. There are "gators" in the bayou, but people still swim there because the reptiles are known to be shy of humans. The big problem for the bayou residents isn't alligators, but rather the land developers who own the property bordering the bayou and plan soon to build housing all along the shore, threatening to evict the houseboat people with their meager homes. There is no thought of forming an association to establish the houseboaters' rights. For one thing, the dwellings are illegal in this bayou. And the fact that neither rent nor taxes are paid leaves the residents with no grounds on which to make their case. It is only a matter of time before these simple houseboats are removed or destroyed.

South of New Orleans are the small towns of Barataria and Lafitte. Fascinating bayou country, very rural in atmosphere. But no houseboats, apparently, except for an unusual floating structure — a large, all-metal, brightly painted, two-story dredge tender. It is a houseboat in the sense that a crew of ten to twelve men live on it for about 20 days at a time, when it accompanies the main dredge on offshore projects. The men who work the dredges also spend a lot of time around the dockyard, repairing and maintaining the equipment. Several of the crew live on the dredge tender steadily. It is home for them.

Westward from New Orleans toward the Bell River is a small town, Pierre Part, on a peaceful bayou of the same name. Outside the town, on this bayou, are several charming little "shoe box"–type houseboats. They are not remarkable in themselves, but the bayou setting tends to enhance their appearance. This seems to be true throughout this part of the country.

Near Pierre Part, the sprawling Bell River is the location of dozens of small, poor, and boxy houseboats shrouded by a variety of huge semi-tropical trees along the riverside. These plain dwellings are inhabited by lower-class working people and their families. Most of the houseboats have electricity, but a surprising number do not. None has running water; and all discharge their waste directly into the river. The structures are supported on simple barge bases, primitive pontoons, or oil drums. Debris of all sorts lies on the adjacent shores. Scruffy houseboats in a gorgeous natural setting.

Northward from the Bell River, in the direction of Baton Rouge, one can see many small clusters of unremarkable houseboats — at places like Bayou Pigeon, Grand Bayou, and Bayou Goula. Farther on, however, along a particularly placid and rustic waterway, Bayou Sorrell, there are two exceptional-looking houseboats. One, called *Vat 69*, is a converted tugboat, floating almost camouflaged under a hood of dense green trees. The second, a few miles north, is *Pancho*, another converted tug, still functional, and inhabited by a single young man who works on this pristine bayou. He made it quite clear that he would not care to live anywhere else.

Right: exterior and master bedroom of a luxury houseboat at West End Park in New Orleans. In the large bedroom on the upper level, the bed is intricately, but securely, suspended by a network of thin metal cables. The 20 × 45 foot floating home was designed and built by the owner, completed in 1971. The houseboat is valued at about $85,000.

Near the town of Lafitte, Louisiana, is this all-metal, brightly colored vessel which is home for a crew of Southern dredgers. The boat spends most of its time moored in this small lagoon, but travels out to its work locations, accompanying the main dredge, for approximately 20 days at a time. It is 20 × 40 feet, and 16 feet high. The crew of ten to twelve men have individual rooms on the upper deck. Below is the main deck, consisting of kitchen, dining room, TV room, and living room.

A typically scenic view of the serene, semi-tropical setting for bayou houseboats near Pierre Part, Louisiana.

Two Louisiana houseboats, splendidly framed by characteristic Southern bayous, trees, and skies, on Bayou Sorrell, not far from Baton Rouge. Both houseboats are converted tugs.

The ultimate in contrast—a tin-roofed bayou houseboat in the midst of a quiet wilderness, rudely interrupted by a U.S. interstate highway, complete with tractor-trailer truck roaring overhead. The bayou is a tributary of the Pearl River, near the border of Mississippi.

Hong Kong

Hong Kong is famous for the beauty of its main harbor, populated with junks that seem as traditional as the Chinese culture itself. The harbor is rendered still more dramatic by the jungle of high-rise office buildings set against a background of steep, rising mountains, often capped by misty clouds. It's no wonder that fishermen and their families are so often found standing atop their junks at sunset, watching the late-day colors playing off the hills, the buildings, and the rich wood of their floating homes.

All of the houseboats in Hong Kong are junks — more than 13,000 of them housing over 65,000 people. Some are large, measuring up to 75 feet in length, and the smallest are around 20 feet long. All assume the same general shape — pointed bows and high, jutting sterns, fashioned after Portuguese and Dutch galleons that sailed the Chinese waters as early as the sixteenth century.

Here, in the harbor of Hong Kong, houseboat owners can enjoy a steady supply of fresh food from sampans providing a menu of fish, rice, drinks, and often complete dinners accompanied by traditional music.

There are a handful of Westerners living on converted junks on Hong Kong Island. One family with four children lives on a large traditional Chinese junk (68 × 22 feet), modernized, or "Americanized," around 1970. Valued at $50,000 it is moored at the Royal Hong Kong Yacht Club, a well-known private marina on the waterfront of downtown Hong Kong. The boat, *Concerto,* is made of pegged (no nails) teakwood, with windows around its sides for the greatest possible light and ventilation. Its electricity is supplied by a generator which charges large batteries powering a refrigerator, washer/dryer, hot-water heater, stereo, TV, and lights. Bottled gas is used for the stove. The boat has three bedrooms, three baths, an open front deck, a shaded back deck, and a lounge in the wheelhouse (p.52).

For hundreds of years, Chinese fishermen and their families have lived on junks. When not fishing at sea, the boats are moored together in huge, often dramatic, clusters (p.60). The families are generally poor, but do not feel themselves disadvantaged. They work hard, live and eat simply, take good care of their junks, and are extremely friendly with their neighbors.

Junks are not particularly stable. Their hulls are flat-bottomed, and their high decks make them quite top-heavy. They are constructed of any of several types of wood. Most favored is teak, because of its density, hardness, and long life in water. Other woods used are rosewood and yacal.

The children are literally born on junks and take to life on the water as naturally as most children live on land. Infants are usually harnessed to masts and railings until they are old enough to know the dangers of the water. Although junk livers depend on the sea for their livelihood, they generally fear the water and do not enjoy swimming. Still, all bathing is done in the water, and children and teenagers are often seen frolicking around the sides of their junks, holding on to ropes tied to the boats.

The fishermen usually spend three to four days between fishing trips tied up in any of Hong Kong's several harbors and typhoon shelters. Then the junks, powered by strong diesel engines (usually two, each 150 or 200 horsepower), make their way to the fishing waters of the China Sea on trips lasting from three days to two weeks. Sails are used to supplement the engines when winds are ideal. Usually, however, only engine power is used on the fishing trips. Normal cruising speed is 15 to 20 knots per hour.

When fish are caught, they are usually placed in special compartments in the hold which allow the seawater to pass through, keeping the fish alive and fresh until the boat reaches Hong Kong, where the catch is sold.

School-age children normally do not go on the fishing trips. They stay with relatives on shore and are required by the government to attend school. But whenever the junks are in port, the children happily join their families for the three- or four-day layover before the next fishing trip.

The biggest danger in junk living is the typhoon. These periodic storms can carry peak winds of 120 miles per hour and easily wipe out a fleet of junks if they are not safely inside a typhoon shelter or lashed together while at sea (hence, junks tend to fish in groups).

Although there is no mooring charge for junks in Hong Kong, they must all be registered with the government. There are several requirements for a fisherman owning a junk. One is the fishing license fee, ranging from $10 to $60 per year, depending on the size of the boat. Another is the mandatory semi-annual dry-docking to have the bottom scraped. Since most of the fishing waters are considered to be Red China's, junk owners must get official permission from the People's Republic, and although this permission is free of charge, each junk is periodically required to give a portion of its catch to the mainland government and attend a communist indoctrination session at special fishing communes set up along the China coast.

One's first view of junks in Hong Kong is likely to be at Causeway Bay, right in the central district of the city, adjacent to the Royal Hong Kong Yacht Club. There are approximately 750 junks housing over 2,000 people in this typhoon shelter.

On the southwest side of the island is the fishing village of Aberdeen, perhaps the most famous spot in the world for junks. There are 20,000 people living on 3,000 junks in Aberdeen Harbor alone, filling the waters with a stunning array of colors, shapes, and sizes.

One can rent a small sampan and be guided in and out of the maze of junks — a good way to get a close-up view of the very friendly and inquisitive people. The odor of fresh cooking is everywhere. Smoke rises from primitive wood stoves where tea is always brewing. Children and adults alike seem to enjoy their compacted environment. The youngsters wave and chant, "Herro, herro," as their popular Western greeting. The women smile shyly and look away as one passes. The men are more forward. They ask, by simple gesturing, to have their pictures taken.

Not far from Hong Kong's central district is Shau Kei Wan, originally a pirates' haunt, and today Hong Kong's second-largest protected harbor for junks. It is here that many junks are constructed and outfitted for fishing. A large-sized junk, say 75 × 22 feet, costs around $40,000 to buy (including the two diesel engines). The average life expectancy of a junk is 30 to 40 years, but some in Hong Kong are as old as 50 years.

The living area on a junk is usually a large central space over the stern, with a ceiling no more than four to five feet high. This room is used for most household functions — sleeping, eating, meeting, etc. When at sea, the average large junk carries nine to eleven workers, usually all blood relations. They sleep on mats on the floor of the main room or on the deck if weather permits. Few junks have private rooms or compartments. Cooking is done on the deck or in an open-roofed corner of the main living area. Fresh food is usually purchased on land and brought to the junk in a sampan. But there are also many small vending boats offering a wide selection of canned and bottled supplies.

The Portuguese colony of Macao, a pleasant boat ride away from Hong Kong, is another gathering place for junks. The main harbors are not as populated as those of Hong Kong, and the junks therefore do not have the kind of impact of the thousands tied together in a place like Aberdeen. Macao is famous for its modern gambling casinos which stand in high contrast to the otherwise poverty-stricken colony. At a little-known Ming Dynasty temple, built around 600 years ago, the most interesting Macao junks can be seen. These are carved and painted houseboats on two of the temple's ornamental rocks. The temple, called "Makok," was once the prayer center for fishermen in days when Macao was more prosperous and its waters abounded with junks.

Two views of traditional Chinese junks bathed in the late-afternoon light at Causeway Bay in Hong Kong Harbor. The modern high-rise buildings and hills behind set off the splendid teak working houseboats.

Exterior of and wheelhouse lounge (looking aft) of the *Concerto,* a modernized junk and home for an American family. Moored at the Royal Hong Kong Yacht Club, the 68 × 22 foot boat was renovated, or "Americanized," around 1970. It carries storage batteries that are charged by a generator, supplying power for hot water, washer/dryer, stereo, television, and smaller electrical appliances. Bottled gas is used for the stove. The junk features three bedrooms, three bathrooms, a roofed rear deck, wheelhouse lounge, and an open front deck.

In Macao, a colony west of Hong Kong leased to the Portuguese by the People's Republic of China, we see a cluster of junks in a background setting of Chinese mainland hills.

A

At Shau Kei Wan, outside central Hong Kong, there is still another huge community of junks. *A:* a typical row against a background of hills, set off here by low-flying jet plane. *B:* an old woman sits in her sampan alongside a resting junk. *C:* interior low-ceilinged living space, showing rich teakwood finish and small sleeping compartments through sliding door. Most of the family/crew, however, sleeps on the open floor.

C

B

A

B

A: on the top deck of a junk, a few members of a typical fishing family relax between trips. *B:* a common sight in Hong Kong's harbors — children playing in the water alongside their boats. *C:* new junk under construction. *D:* vending barge, servicing hundreds of surrounding junks. The owners live aboard.

C

D

Neatly aligned group of five junks tied up at
Causeway Bay, Hong Kong Harbor. The tarps are
used to protect cargo and shade the decks from the
intense sunlight.

Portside view of Aberdeen junk, with sunshade spread open and decorative flags fluttering in a rare breeze during the Hong Kong summer.

A Macao junk decorated traditionally for a wedding ceremony. Note refreshment cart in foreground.

Several hundred of the thousands of clustered junks in famous Aberdeen Harbor on Hong Kong Island. In the background, one sees the steady traffic of junks leaving for or returning from their fishing trips.

Thailand

For centuries Bangkok, the capital of Thailand, was considered the Venice of the East. It was all canals, with no streets, until the early part of the twentieth century. Thailand has a long tradition of boating and houseboat living. Originally, Thai thinking was influenced by the Chinese concept of a boat as both a house and a means of trade. On the large rivers and small canals alike, this life-style still prevails as cargo-houseboats move steadily on the waterways.

Bangkok has a large, serpentine river running through its center, the Chao Phraya. Branching off this river, which continues to run north and south of Bangkok, are many narrow canals, known as "klongs," along which a variety of houseboats are located. The smaller ones, especially along the klongs in central Bangkok, rarely move. They serve as part of a marketplace, selling a variety of goods at their moorage along the banks, particularly fresh green vegetables and fruits in season. Other staples are sold, such as rice, coal, peanuts, and various dry goods. The city's klong boats are poor, and, at least on the outside, in disrepair. The klongs themselves are stagnant, with water that has turned black from years of residue and sewage. In certain places the stench is almost too strong to bear.

But, surprisingly, the insides of the houseboats—the living quarters—are neat, well-kept, and quite clean. The teak floors are polished diligently; pots, pans, basins, and other cookware are scoured and stored neatly; freshly laundered clothes are hung daily in the sun to dry.

On one such canal within Bangkok's city limits, Klong Maha Nak, there are hundreds of these market boats jammed together in a row perhaps half a mile long (p.70). The inhabitants are poor families, living in seeming squalor, but apparently healthy and content with their modest businesses and way of life. While parents are selling their goods, infants can be seen napping in cribs or hammocks, tended by grandparents, who keep the living quarters clean, sew and weave, and prepare food.

Fresh water is bought from vendors cruising the banks with barrels of water strapped to their hand trucks. The water is syphoned into large, ornate earthenware crocks on the decks of the houseboats. Electricity is available to the boats through shoreside lines, not more sophisticated than ordinary extension cords. One of the main uses for the power is to run electric fans, used steadily in the extreme heat to cool sleeping children and adults.

Most klong houseboats are small in size, about 30 to 35 feet long, as compared to their twice-larger cousins on the Chao Phraya River. They are hooded with corrugated tin, often rusty. And many of the boats cover the tin with canvas tarps for increased protection from the scorching sun.

To many people, especially the Bangkok authorities, these klong boats are an eyesore; and the klongs themselves are dangerously polluted. The Thai government has instituted a program to move the boats, but the tradition of the marketplace is strong, and

the program has therefore been difficult to implement. Once in a while a houseboat is forced to move from its mooring, but invariably the boat returns after a short time.

There are many rural klongs outside Bangkok. A typical one, Klong Rangsit, is in a setting reminiscent of the Louisiana bayous. Along the canal, which parallels a two-lane highway, are many charming small houseboats. In the narrow space between the klong and the road, small huts are erected in front of the houseboats to display and sell a variety of dry goods, groceries, and fresh produce. The fruit and vegetables are bought from surrounding farms, delivered to the canalside huts in cars and trucks, and then retailed to local townspeople or passing cars on the road.

The rural canals, apart from serving as a permanent base for houseboats, are also used to irrigate farmland. The waterways here are beautiful and refreshingly clean compared to Bangkok's canals. The surface of the water is covered with a prolific bright green waterplant called "java" (pronounced "yawah"), which was imported from Java by Thailand's King Rama V in the mid-nineteenth century. Often the floating plants blossom with lovely purple flowers.

The houseboats along Klong Rangsit are moved infrequently, perhaps once every five years. The people genuinely enjoy their boats and the pleasant natural surroundings. Their children attend nearby schools, many transported by narrow "long-tail" boats, which are scull-type water taxis driven by powerful outboard motors (converted from car engines) with long, tail-like rudders specially adapted to the shallow waters of Thailand's canals.

Family life on the klong is centered on the living unit, the houseboat. There is always some chore to do, whether cleaning, washing, or cooking. The entire family pitches in with a light and jolly spirit, a sense of play, often accompanied by traditional songs and chants.

North of Bangkok, in the vicinity of Ayutthaya, former capital of Thailand (1350–1767), the river Chao Phraya bustles with large cargo-houseboats. The typical vessel has a deep wooden hull with rounded bow and stern, huge rudder, and hooded roof made of corrugated tin. There are front and rear open decks partitioned from the interior cargo section by sturdy, watertight doors. When the boat is filled with heavy cargo it sinks quite low in the water, flooding the fore and aft decks and giving the effect that the boat has actually sunk (p.64). The families living on the boat move inside the cargo area when the decks are flooded. If it is soft cargo, like sacks of rice, people sleep right on top of it. If the cargo is hard, like bricks, extra room must be reserved in the cargo area for sleeping on the floor. When empty, these cargo boats sit quite high on the water (p.64). They look their best in this state, for one can see the rich colors of the teakwood, the traditional red-orange and aquamarine painted trim, and the impressive ornamented rudder.

The other style of cargo-houseboat is the very large, deep-hulled barge, with a closed or open living area built as a superstructure on top of its deck (p.66).

Some Thai boats are in full use for as long as 30 years. Most of those seen on the river, however, are less than ten years old. The boats move north and south on the Chao Phraya according to the seasonal availability of various cargos, trading and selling first in one region, then another. Typical cargos are coconuts, rice, sand (for concrete), pottery, bricks, and fresh produce of all kinds.

Relatively few cargo boats have their own engines. Most are hauled up and down the river in caravans ranging from two to fifteen boats. They are pulled by small, decorative tugboats whose size seems hardly adequate for the great weights they are hauling (p.65).

Most of the owners of cargo-houseboats also have homes on land (unlike the Chinese). These modest homes on the banks of the river, many built on stilts, are used only a few days at a time as resting places between river trips. Adult members of the families generally go on the hauling trips while their children live along the riverside with relatives, and attend school. The youngsters love to frolic in the river and seem to be excellent swimmers. One of their favorite games is swimming out to the center of the river, where the current is strong, and being carried various distances downstream. They then grab onto the ropes between boats in a moving caravan to get a "free lift" back up the river. The sight is delightful, as groups of young boys and girls have a sort of whirlpool bath, water streaming along their tan bodies as they are pulled up river.

Another, different, area of the Chao Phraya is near the town of Prachan, south of Bangkok. The river is quite wide, perhaps a mile. There seems to be more traffic and heavier commerce here than in the Ayutthaya region. It is almost like a harbor. Navy ships are spread along the piers, and seemingly endless numbers of cargo-houseboats move along the river and dot the shores as well. There are many more of the large, barge-type boats with living structure on top than the round, tin-roofed variety. In the background is the famous Oriental Hotel, a modern high-rise building providing a vivid contrast with its neighboring traditional buildings, nearby temples, and sunbaked wooden houseboats on the water.

Farther down the river is a quiet inlet with a caravan colony at rest. The houseboats don't look like trading boats here. They seem rather like proud and peaceful homes, some next to each other, nestled into the rich greenery of the banks, and others alone, independent, and quietly resting on the still waters away from the river's busy current. One boat, with polished teak decks, was holding a fair-sized cargo of rice. The owner, a man looking much younger than his years, sat under the tin roof of the bow deck, weaving a basket, relaxing in his house between trips (p.65).

Not a sunken boat, this vessel is loaded to capacity with cargo. Water floods the small deck areas at the bow and stern, but is kept from the cargo by watertight doors. The crew, usually the owner and family members, eat and sleep inside the boat, on or around the cargo.

An immaculately kept all-teak Thai houseboat on the bank of the Chao Phraya River, near Bangkok. Its hull empty, this typical cargo boat, with its corrugated tin roof, sits quite high on the water.

A cargo of rice in sacks occupies the hulls of this working houseboat, not quite fully loaded. In the foreground is a wooden sleeping platform, with straw bedroll to the left. At the far end of the vessel, the owner contentedly weaves a straw basket.

One of the hundreds of cargo caravans that can be seen daily, pulled up and down the Chao Phraya River by small, charmingly decorated, and powerful tugboats.

Two examples of the largest type of live-on cargo boat found on Thailand's rivers. *A:* the more typical living area on this kind of boat is the open-sided shelter with makeshift roof. *B:* cargo-less, and standing handsomely against the sky, this boat has a complete, enclosed living unit on its top deck, with a lower roofed area over the stern.

A

B

Outside Bangkok, on a rural canal called Klong Rangsit, a medium-sized cargo houseboat is moored along the banks of a rustic village. Next to it, a "long-tail" boat, filled with white-shirted children, serves as a water taxi, returning the children home from school.

Two canalside vending boats along Klong Rangsit, with its bright java (yawah) plants floating. These small houseboats do not move around much, but serve as homes and storage for various goods. Klong Rangsit runs parallel to a narrow highway which the boat owners use to transport their wares by truck or car to their boats. The selling is done in small sheds between the highway and the klong.

A hunkering woman cooks food aboard her small-sized houseboat located at a temple village along the river.

In the jammed-up Klong Maha Nak in central
Bangkok, hundreds of permanently moored
marketplace houseboats line the canal's banks.
Owned by poor merchants, the smallish boats
accommodate entire families. Like the larger river
cargo boats, these old vessels have passed from
one generation to another.

A mother proudly displays two infants on the stern of her tiny abode.

In a somewhat more prosperous boat, a grandmother embroiders while caring for her grandchildren. Note the electric fan, so popular with these hardworking families in the unbearable summer heat and humidity of Bangkok.

Kashmir

The Vale of Kashmir is considered by many to be one of the most beautiful places in the world. It is in an area officially called the State of Jammu and Kashmir, in the most northern portion of India. The seat of the capital moves every six months. In the cold months (October to March) it is in the city of Jammu in the south; and in the remaining months in Srinagar, up north.

Srinagar, a large, spread-out city, is built around bustling Dal Lake and the curving River Jelhum. Dal Lake is connected by a series of canals to the more rural and serene Nagin Lake, surrounded by the towering, snowcapped Himalayas.

From the top of Shankracharya Mountain, the highest point in central Srinagar and the site of the Shiv Jee Temple, one can see in a spectacular 360-degree panorama both lakes, the serpentine river, the entire city, and the majestic mountains. Looking down onto the various waterways, one sees the famous "hotel houseboats," some aligned in long, straight rows on the shores of the city, others isolated in entirely rustic settings. There are also the "dungas" and "bahats," native houseboats, lining the canals and spread along the lakeshores and river banks.

The famous Kashmiri hotel houseboats are rectangular, ranging in size from about 30 × 10 feet to 125 × 20 feet. They are rated in five categories—deluxe, first class, second class, etc. The deluxe hotels are the largest. They are made of devdar, a sturdy, dense Indian hardwood similar to teak. The railings along the top sun deck, front porch deck, and stairway to the water (where the visitor is let off and picked up by water taxi) are intricately carved from the same type of wood. The full-length sun deck has a patterned awning over part of it to provide shade, and the porch and windows of the boat are also decoratively curtained and awninged (p.82). Entering the deluxe houseboat from the porch, one steps into a huge (30 × 20 foot) sitting room, decorated with handmade Indian rugs, hand-carved natural wood ceilings and paneled walls, rich-textured curtains, and finely carved and polished chairs, sofas, desks, and tables (p.82). Aft of the dining room is a narrow passageway, off which is a kitchen pantry, stairs leading to the sun deck, and three private bedrooms, each with its own bath and toilet, with hot and cold running water.

A tourist renting the deluxe houseboat is given three full meals a day (choice of Indian or Continental cuisine), served by a 24-hour manservant, or valet, who sleeps or sits in the pantry when not working, and is always on hand to advise about tours, shopping, and the manners and customs of Kashmir. Food is usually prepared onshore by the houseboat's own chef, then brought on board to be served.

The going rate for the deluxe model is around $10 per person per day, food and service included. First- and second-class hotel houseboats usually provide the same services and cuisine, but are smaller in size with only one or two bedrooms. They may not have hot water, and the condition of the boat itself and the furnishings may not be as good as on the deluxe. The daily rates for these boats are from $6 to $8. The smallest houseboat hotels, with one bed-

room, may be rented for as little as $3 a day, not including food, service, or hot water. They may be a little run-down, but they are usually clean and very charming in their decor. Most of the houseboat hotels are clustered together on Dal Lake, in the central section of Srinagar (p.74). Others are spaced out on Nagin Lake, in the shadow of the great Himalaya Mountains—a setting of breathtaking beauty (p.84-85).

Each houseboat hotel has its name on a painted sign over the porch. It is interesting to pass the various rows and observe the names of the houseboat hotels, reflecting a kind of affection for the Western tourist, American and English in particular. Some of the U.S.-related names are: *A. Jazz, Holiday Inn, Kashmir Hilton, White House, Jacqueline, Cherry Stone, Bostan* [sic], *New Texas, New Manhattan, Young Montana,* and *U.S.A.* Among the English-inspired names are: *Derby Shire, Savoy Hotel, H.M.S. Pinafore, Duke of Windsor, Buckingham Palace, Miss England,* and *Happy England.* Still other houseboats have general names, such as *Pigeon, Retreet* [sic], *Noah's Ark, Heavensun,* and *New Zenith.*

The hotel houseboats in the idyllic Vale of Kashmir are an old tradition. One family owning about eight houseboats has collected letters of appreciation from visitors—ambassadors, writers, missionaries, politicians, industrialists, and other dignitaries—for more than a century. The owner has framed a letter addressed to his father from U.S. President Theodore Roosevelt, extolling the beauties of Kashmir and the superb appearance and service of the houseboat he rented there.

The word "tourist" has not taken on bad connotations with the Kashmiri people, who have proudly hosted Westerners for many years. Srinagar is dependent on tourism for much of its income. The crafts, artifacts, rugs, furniture, and clothing produced there are expertly made, and sold (bargained for) at quite reasonable prices by Western standards. Thousands of independent Kashmiris rely on this trade for their livelihood.

Srinagar does not have an international airport and can only be reached by local and not always reliable flights, from places like New Delhi and Bombay. Because of this inconvenience, Kashmir has never been overrun with tourists. Nor has Srinagar been exploited by large hotel chains, commercial restaurants, or modern land developers—as have so many other, once simple, beauty spots in the world.

The Kashmiri people are therefore "unspoiled" in their relationship with Westerners. They quite sincerely wish to make the visitor comfortable, to extend their hospitality. And they ask in return not much more than a measure of appreciation. Even the rower of a water taxi wants to feel he has satisfied his passenger. The most commonly used expression of politeness is "As it pleases you, sir," applied to most every situation, as "Thank you" is in the West.

The lakes and canals around Srinagar are not monopolized by hotels on the water. There are two other types of houseboats, and these are used only by Kashmiri natives (though a small colony of

European and American hippies stay for months at a time on native houseboats, paying very low rents and enjoying the abundance of hashish). One type, the dunga, is used for living only. Most are inhabited by working-class families. Typically, they work on land in small businesses, shops, banks, government offices. Some work on the water, either as "shikara" (water taxi) drivers, or vendors in "demawaris" (small flat boats) selling a wide variety of goods to both tourists and natives on or around the waterways. Their wares include fur hats and gloves, scarfs, shirts, suits, leather jackets, embroidered bedspreads, cutlery, dry goods, candy, soda, beer, snacks, and so forth.

Dungas, like the larger bahats and the hotel houseboats, are made from devdar wood. They are generally low structures, averaging 25 feet in length. They look very much like small land houses built onto low, flat boat hulls. They have several rooms and the windows are actually sliding wood panels. Sections of the roof are built as flaps which can be raised somewhat for ventilation (p.78). Some of the dungas are painted and others are ornamented with carved panels. Most, however, are left plain, their natural wood gradually getting sunbleached to soft shades of gray, yellow, and brown. Dungas are the most popular type of houseboat in Srinagar. They are tied, more or less permanently, to the shores of both Nagin and Dal lakes, to the dense foliage along the winding canals, and to the stone banks of the River Jelhum. They have no electricity or running water. Light is provided by candles or kerosene lamps, and all washing is done in the water on which they rest. Sewage is dumped into these same waters, and despite the obvious lack of sanitation, this condition has prevailed for many generations without notable sickness or disease.

The largest native Kashmiri houseboat, the bahat, is a cargo boat used to haul wood, stones, bricks, sand, or mud from one village to another, almost entirely on the River Jelhum. Bahats are about 40 feet long. Much of the front half, either enclosed or open, is used for its cargo, while the living area is only on the rear half of the boat. The house-like structures resemble those of the dunga, but the roof flaps only open a few inches. Sometimes there is a flat open deck atop the living space (p.79). When loaded, the bahat sinks quite low in the water. The hull seems to disappear and one gets the impression that an ordinary house is floating down the river, as if swept off land by a flood.

Neither dungas nor bahats are powered by engines of any sort. All moving is patiently and skillfully accomplished by paddling or poling (p.76). It is particularly fascinating to watch the loaded bahats being maneuvered by an entire family against the sometimes tricky river currents. The dungas and bahats are a rather special part of the Kashmir scenery. At dawn and dusk they somehow manage to reflect almost unimaginable shades of the sky and water. And in the heat of midday their wooden hulls show a spectrum of warm, flesh-like colors.

One other type of Kashmiri boat is used for living, but it is quite difficult to call it a houseboat. It is the "gadawari," a fisherman's boat in the exact style of the small, flat demawari used for selling goods on the waterways. In boats no longer than 15 feet — without any structure built on, but only tent-like flaps of straw mats or canvas tarps — whole families work, eat, and sleep. Groups of five or six families tie up together each evening along the tree-lined banks of the canals. There, they cook and eat together, adults playing with and singing to their children. It is a scene of touching communal harmony. The families are quite poor. They do not aspire to owning a dunga or bahat. They fish with small nets in the lakes and canals.

When Westerners pass by the various houseboats in Srinagar, the people invariably smile, often waving. Children chant a traditional rhyme: *"Mimi salaam, pat pat gulam,"* which roughly translated means "(Western) lady, hello, you have servants following you." The banks of the lakes and river are, it seems, always populated with adults and children, washing clothes, bathing, singing, and playing in the water. Adult women are shy and coy. They smile, but then turn away or cover their faces with the traditional Indian veil. On their dungas, where they often lean out their windows to wash pots and pans, they will smile at the passerby, but then duck back inside and slam their wooden windows until the stranger moves on (p.78). Some, less shy, will give the traditional greeting, *"Asalaam alaykum,"* "peace to you."

The Vale of Kashmir is an inspiring place. The people, rich or poor, seem to love their traditional ways. They welcome tourists not at all because they wish to become "Westernized," but rather to share their customs and hospitality, to trade or sell their splendid crafts.

Temples dot the banks of the River Jelhum, and on some nights worshippers can be heard across the waters chanting for hours on end. The many Kashmiri children are noticeably adored and pampered by their parents. Everyone has an accepted role in life — usually within the family's tradition. Ambition is still thought to be an undesirable trait. Yet curiosity about the Western world grows with each generation, and a certain amount of capitalism is taking root.

The great Vale of Kashmir as seen from the top of Shankracharya Mountain at the Shiv Jee Temple. Dal Lake with its hundreds of hotel houseboats is in the foreground. In the middle distance is a fortress-covered hill overlooking central Srinagar. And in the distance, through the great valley's haze, are the Himalayas.

Group of cargo-carrying bahats, or loading boats, on the River Jelhum in front of a complex of archaic apartment dwellings.

A dunga, or private houseboat, being poled along one of Dal Lake's canals.

Front of an old and colorful dunga, moored alongside a large bahat with house-like structure next to its open top deck.

Two typical dungas, seen against steeply rising private apartments.

Newly finished dunga, not yet weather-beaten, with characteristic sliding panels open for ventilation.

Sun-bleached dungas moored on a Srinagar canal. The boat at right has the ventilation flap on its roof in open position.

Two Srinagar women on a demawari (flat open boat), stopping to chat with a third woman on her dunga.

Row of large bahats, with near-empty cargo areas in front, are tied up along a canal. The family on the second boat is sharing a hookah pipe.

Colony of gadawaris, or fishermen's houseboats, settling for the evening along the rustic bank of a canal between Dal Lake and Nagin Lake. The families on these tiny, tarp-covered flat boats all sleep aboard in very limited spaces.

The strong shadows of late afternoon dramatize the primitive beauty of this scene, in which a lone oarsman maneuvers his bahat along a Srinagar canal.

A tidy row of shikaras, gaily colored water taxis, awaiting their next customers. Note English-language names and advertisements of "spring seats."

On the River Jelhum, two bahats are moored alongside one of the many gold-domed temples gracing the river's shores.

A

B

C

Left: exterior and two interior views of the *New Zenith*, a luxury-class floating hotel in central Srinagar. *A:* elegantly appointed living room with wood paneling, carved ceiling and furniture, and Indian carpets. *B:* dining room adjoining the living room. *C:* all decked out with awnings, curtains, and rooftop canopy. Note front porch with steps leading to the water to accommodate the shikaras bringing passengers to and from the boat.

A: afternoon sun projects moving water patterns on the carved ceiling of this Srinagar hotel's porch. *B:* sparkling whites, blacks, and silvers decorate the famous hotels on Dal Lake.

A

B

Two indescribable sunset views of romantic Nagin Lake's houseboat hotels, dwarfed by the foothills of the Himalayas.

France

France, particularly the waterways in and around Paris, is well known for its houseboats. They are the long, narrow "péniches," or working barges. In an area known as "Circonscription de Port Autonome de Paris," which is a 40-mile belt around Paris, there are approximately 300 péniches used for living, and some for living-and-working. In central Paris, on the Seine, there are an estimated 80 péniche-type houseboats.

The majority of these boats were built between 1925 and 1935, and were used originally to haul various raw materials along the intricate waterways of France. Flat-bottomed, with powerful engines, they are remarkably maneuverable through narrow canals, under bridges, and around corners. The standard-sized péniche is 125 × 16 feet. Its hold, the cargo area, is either open throughout or divided into five or six large compartments corresponding to the sliding roof hoods that protect the cargo (p.91). The original living compartments occupy the rearmost 20 to 25 feet of the boat, beneath the traditional barge wheelhouse. Using space efficiently, the living compartment has no more than two rooms (usually one), with bunks built around the sides. The kitchen/pantry is off to one side. Toilets are the traditional nautical "pump johns" that discharge waste directly into the river. Water is stored in tanks, or, when the boat is moored, is run on through a hose. Electricity is supplied from a generator powered by the engine, or else from extension lines run from an available land source when the boat is tied up.

Working péniches (there are 5,000 in the whole of France) can be seen every day on the Seine. In the past few decades there has been a trend to convert the older péniches into full-blown houseboats—all 100 feet of their loft-like holds. Today a raw (non-converted) péniche in good condition, with a clean hull and working engine, costs 40,000 francs, or approximately $8,000.

Converting the long cargo space into living space is an expensive process, usually costing, as a minimum, the same price as that of the raw boat. But when the conversion is complete, the time and effort are usually found to be more than worthwhile (p.91). Not many apartments in Paris are anywhere near the size of péniches.

Legally, the houseboats in the Seine are allowed to moor in specified places along the banks for one month at a time. This law is rarely enforced, however, and most péniches stay docked for indefinite periods of time. Péniche owners like to use their boats for pleasure cruising, but it is a risky business owing to the likelihood of losing one's moorage space to another péniche, even if the cruise is for a few hours.

The government, through the Port of Paris Authority, has been trying to pressure péniche owners to pay taxes for mooring on the Seine. The "habitation flottante," as the Port calls it, should be considered a house, and, like any other house on (or using) Paris property, should be taxed. Houseboat taxes would be determined by the size of the vessel. The government is not unsympathetic to the péniche owners. However, they fear an overcrowding of the Seine if the houseboats are not taxed in such a way as to keep their numbers limited. (In recent years the Port Authority has been mounting a huge economic program to make Paris a "port"—inviting national and international merchant vessels to increase commerce by trading and selling in Paris' many dockyards. It is in the Port's interest to keep the Seine as unclogged as possible.)

In 1975, the most recent of several houseboat associations was formed to protect the rights of those living in péniches. Called "Association de Défense de l'Habitat Fluvial," the organization has proposed a plan by which reasonable taxes would be paid, as moorage fees, in return for facilities supplying water, electricity, and sewage. (The péniche owners would also pay for the amount of utilities consumed.) Several proposals and counter-proposals have been exchanged by the Port Authority and the Association since 1975, but no resolution has yet been reached. Both sides seem relaxed and casual about the final solution to the Paris houseboat problem. The Port Authority has not yet completed "a number of studies on houseboats," and the Association is working toward unity of its membership on the issue of what is "a fair tax" for services and the security of their moorages.

It is mostly the younger boat owners who comprise the Association. Described as "individualists, not hippies" by the Port Authority, the modern péniche owners are characteristically active and creative young people, many with families, who do indeed feel their individualism expressed through houseboat living. They work as painters, sculptors, writers, architects, craftspeople, musicians, illustrators, teachers, and "independents"—those who have enough money to last a few years and simply enjoy the daily routine of tending their houseboats in the heart of their romantic city.

A minority of péniche owners in Paris are the retired captains (and families) who once used their boats in the work for which they were designed—carrying cargo. They live quietly amid the new generation of Paris houseboat people. Many of the retired still use only the péniche's original rear quarters as living space. They don't need the huge area of their hold, which may be used for storage only.

Along the Seine, facing Quai Conti, is an eye-stopping houseboat. It is not a French péniche, but a seagoing Dutch cargo boat, an "Oostzee-tjalk" (p. 89). Named *Souqui*, it was built in 1890 in Groningen, Holland. Until 1935 its sole function was carrying cargo between Indonesia and Europe via the Cape of Good Hope.

Retired in 1935, *Souqui* was bought by an Englishman who converted it to a pleasure craft and lived on it until 1942, when it was conscripted by the English military and used as a transport for the duration of World War II. Following that, the boat was bought by a wealthy Dutch wine merchant, who is responsible for the basic interior design as it looks today. *Souqui* passed through the hands of several owners from different countries during the fifties, sixties, and early seventies. In 1974 it was bought by the present owner and sailed to France, where it has since been lived on. It is now undergoing a major mechanical, interior, and exterior overhaul, with the intention of making it as seaworthy as it was when first built. The owner hopes to use *Souqui* for international pleasure trips.

At present the exterior of this elegant, antique boat has been refinished in black paint (it was white before), and all the woodwork, including the masts, has been revarnished. The interior is a series of small and middle-sized intimate rooms, rich with textured fabrics, old cushioned sofas, and endless artifacts from years past. All in all, *Souqui* is a visual feast.

In one of Paris' wealthier suburbs, Neuilly, is an unusual colony of *non*-péniche houseboats, moored on a quiet, countrified portion of the Seine, opposite a small islet, Ile du Pont. The 34 houseboats here are unusual for several reasons. One is that they are legal. Rents are paid to the Harbor of Paris, a branch of the city government. In return, the houseboat owners get permanent moorings with shoreside patches of land (usually turned into flower gardens) and city-supplied access to water and electricity. Sanitation is in the form of septic tanks on the boats, supplied by the owner. Rents are based on the size of the houseboat. The average annual rent at Neuilly is about $1,000 (5,000 francs). And the average-sized boat is 15 × 60 feet.

The Neuilly houseboats are varied in design. Some are in the style of large, boxy floating homes; others are converted from luxury cruisers. Most of the residents are fairly affluent businessmen, and some are well known. At one time the famed French "cavalier" actor, Jean Marais, inhabited one of the Neuilly houseboats.

The residents, mostly families, feel special, if not privileged, living on these picturesque houseboats. They are near central Paris, yet hidden in a very rural environment, protected on one side by their gardens and on the other by the heavily wooded Ile du Pont. The little island was once owned privately by a rich sugar mogul, who used it as a weekend retreat. Following the owner's death a few years ago, Ile du Pont was supposed to revert to the City of Paris. But the owner had stipulated some time earlier that it should be reserved for the private use of his faithful gardener. To protect the gardener, who is in his eighties, the city closed off the island from the attached bridge. Only the gardener can enter and leave. When he dies, the city will turn the isle into a public park, not to be changed from its present, completely natural, form.

The dwellers on the Neuilly houseboats look forward to many years of undisturbed beauty in their backyard.

About ten miles west of central Paris is Port Marly, a small town on the Seine. Along the banks are several houseboats, built mostly in the familiar péniche style. But one stands out. There is nothing quite like it elsewhere in France, Europe, or perhaps the world. On an all-concrete hull measuring 130 × 26 feet, the owner, French sculptor Saint-Maur, built his own free-form superstructure out of polyurethane foam applied to a series of shaped-metal armatures. It is a rambling, curved, multi-layered labyrinth of living rooms, studios, storage spaces, and decks.

The boat, along with four or five others, was originally built by French engineers during World War I, and used as an oversized péniche-type transport to haul large cargoes of various materials to and from England.

Saint-Maur has lived on the boat, *La Polybéton*, since 1965, when he began erecting his monumental superstructure. The work took four years to complete, after which the artist could again focus full-time on his own sculpture.

Saint-Maur has been living on houseboats since 1926, when he was 20 years old and first started doing artwork. He believes houseboats make the best studios, providing excellent light for drawing, painting, and sculpture. The *Polybéton* gets — and pays for — its electricity and water from the shoreside. But Saint-Maur laments having to pay ever-increasing taxes "for the right to moor here." He believes, with his wife, that people like himself, known as "marginaux" (marginal types like artists, hippies, and intellectuals, choosing not to be fully integrated with society), should be left to live freely and independently, not exploited by the government or establishment.

Saint-Maur's extraordinary houseboat — a floating sculpture, studio, and home all-in-one — reflects not only the spirit of this pioneer artist, but also that of many other houseboat people, whose boats are their homes as well as expressions of individual taste and style.

Four péniches moored on the Seine, with a familiar Paris landmark in the background.

On the Seine, facing Quai Conti, is the extraordinary *Souqui,* a seagoing Dutch "Oostzee-tjalk," a handsome antique boat now being restored inside and out. *A:* exterior as seen from the stern. *B* and *C:* two interior details showing some of the fascinating furnishings.

B

C

A

Group of péniches moored parallel to each other
along a modern, industrialized area of the Seine.
The second boat from the right is unusual in Paris
for its conspicuous rainbow colors.

Two typical péniches on the Seine. Photo *A* gives
the viewer a good idea of the great length of these
French houseboats. *B:* loft-like interior of the near
péniche in photo *A*. Handmade hooded fireplace
is the centerpiece of this modern sitting area.
Farther along are several antique rocking chairs.
And at the far end are the dining area and kitchen
counters.

B

A

As the Seine wanders through the wealthy Paris suburb of Neuilly, there is a row of thirty-four higher-class houseboats. Some are large floating homes, others are converted barges and luxury cruisers. All are permanently and legally moored along a thickly treed bank. The moorage includes the adjacent land, on which most of the well-to-do owners grow lush flower gardens.

At Port Marly, about ten miles from central Paris, is this extraordinary multi-storied houseboat owned by modern artist Saint-Maur. The superstructure (on a concrete barge base) and free-form interior were designed and built by the artist. *A:* grotto-like sitting area on the middle level of the houseboat. *B:* detail showing sculptured sofa that runs into low portion of the hooded ceiling. *C:* main entrance and sculptured skylighted roof.

A

B

C

England

With over 2,000 miles of inland waterways, numerous harbors, and coastal estuaries, England is said to have an estimated 15,000 to 20,000 people currently living on boats as their permanent residence.

Earliest records of family living aboard British boats are dated around 1800, when a small number of wives and girlfriends of the captains of cargo-carrying "narrow boats" moved aboard during a period of trade and wage cutbacks, in order to save the cost of hired crewmen. Narrow boats are so called because they were built quite long and narrow, about 70 feet × 7 feet, as an efficient means of navigating the numerous, very narrow canals that crisscrossed England. The boats were originally drawn along the canals by horse. Later, with the introduction first of steam engines, then internal-combustion engines, the narrow boat was self-propelling and often towed along a second, motorless, narrow boat called a "butty."

The initiation of women to narrow-boat work and life was considered temporary in 1800, when economic circumstances were unfavorable for the canal cargo carriers. But increasingly it appeared that many of the women enjoyed their newfound maritime life-style and many of the men relished their companionship. Women were to remain on board for generations to come. They added many homey touches to the vessels, most of them utilitarian, but some decorative, such as the painting of murals (landscapes, castles, flowers) on the outer decks and the trimming of rudders, windows, doorways, etc.

As the narrow-boat population increased during the nineteenth century, many canalside businesses sprouted up, specifically to supply and service the floating families. Most daily shopping was done within yards of the towing path. Gradually the narrow boats and their inhabitants took on a unique character and gained a reputation with the general public as an insular subculture with its own trade practices, code of ethics, and life-style. One manifestation of the latter was the common practice of carving, painting, or even embroidering the relatively few possessions they owned and were able to keep in or on their small living spaces (typically 10 × 7 feet). Narrow-boat decoration, in short, became a tradition, one that can still be seen today, owing to a modern revival of narrow-boat living in England.

With the growth of railway systems and overland trucking in the twentieth century, the narrow-boat population dwindled. Only a relative few could be found after World War II. Most had been abandoned and were destroyed by the British Waterways System, which towed them out to sea and sank them.

In recent years there has been new interest in narrow boats. The remaining old ones are being restored. And modern ones are being built by a thriving industry promoting the tradition of narrow-boat living. The original vessels were made with elm keels and riveted iron sides. Today's models are all built in steel, but otherwise conform to the traditional design, with graceful bows and sterns on a long barge base, supporting a box-type superstructure as the living space.

England has many other styles of houseboats, among them Thames College barges, Zulu fishing boats, Dutch flat-bottomed boats or "tjalks," retired naval launches (some of which bear plaques for service at Dunkirk), and modern floating homes. Communities of houseboats may be found all along the Thames and on smaller canals, in harbors and estuaries. Many of today's owners are facing difficulties not dissimilar to those in America and France. They have had to organize, through houseboat associations, to demand their rights as water-dwelling citizens for basic community services, such as sanitation disposal, in return for their taxes and fees. Every English houseboat owner must pay an annual fee to the Water Authority, which licenses the boats for use in the waterways. Then there is the mooring fee, paid to the owner of the land or marina at which the boat is tied up. Finally, there is a kind of "property" tax paid to the local authority or council, in return for garbage and sewage disposal, education, libraries, etc. In past years many of these services were not provided, owing to the vagueness or indeed lack of ordinances pertaining specifically to houseboats — they were simply not recognized. Today, however, as a result of the long and concerted efforts of houseboat associations, the ordinances have been amended, or new ones created, so that most of the basic community needs are now provided by local authorities.

Most established moorage facilities provide toilets on shore, thus alleviating the problem of sewage disposal. But many houseboats have "chemical closets," which are emptied regularly at specific disposal points. Still others flush their waste directly into the water, a practice unacceptable to the authorities, and which is fast disappearing owing to houseboat associations' pressure on individuals to conform to local ordinances and good ecological practice.

Electricity, telephone, and running water are made available to houseboats by arrangement with the appropriate utility companies.

A recent survey of the English houseboat population describes the vocational breakdown as follows: artistic 16%, engineering/technical 16%, managerial/civil service 10%, skilled trades 10%, teacher/nurse/social work 12%, sales/P.R. 9%, clerical 9%, student 4%, unemployed/retired 4%, other 10%. The reasons given for preferring houseboat living to other forms of residency are, in order of choice: river life, interest in boats, economy, privacy/quiet, and community spirit.

These findings, along with others dealing with age and condition of boats, mooring fees, length of time living on houseboats, and age of residents, led the surveyers to the following conclusion: "The modern houseboat dweller is *not* a wandering nomad with no job, living in a badly maintained boat. He is a useful citizen living on the river through his own choice, staying in one place, maintaining his boat, and contributing to society by his work . . . "

In the Chelsea district of central London, near the Battersea Bridge, there is a long row of houseboats converted from or built atop old barges. Some of them, like those in Sausalito, California, are artistically handmade, with natural wood in angular designs. Others at this moorage are straightforward box-type structures simply sitting upon their barge bases. When the river is low all these Chelsea houseboats rest motionless on the silty mud.

North of Chelsea, but well within London's city limits, is the widely known houseboat area called Little Venice. There, several intersecting canals are lined with dozens of houseboats, most of which are in the narrow-boat genre, charmingly painted and decorated. In this area, residents rent not only moorage space but several yards into the adjacent land, on which they grow lovely flower gardens, set up lawn furniture, and often picnic. The price of the houseboats at Little Venice ranges from $5,000 to $17,000, although some have been known to sell for as little as $1,700. Toilets are on the shore, as are garbage cans, which are emptied regularly by the public sanitation department. Water is brought to the boats through hoses attached to taps on land.

Little Venice, being in the midst of a respectable residential area of London, is considered a choice place to live, affording all of the city's advantages, yet isolated by virtue of its protected waterside moorage. The residents enjoy their unconventional living spaces. They enthusiastically maintain their boats, painting this, scraping that, repairing a window or door. Children have no trouble growing up in this "natural" environment within the boundaries of one of the world's largest cities.

As the River Thames winds its way southwest out of London, one finds many sorts of houseboats, some boxy—the size and shape of floating homes—and others converted from sailboats, launches, deep-hulled barges, and old cabin cruisers. In the area of Sunbury is an elegant-looking floating home, the *Astoria*, designed in the festive Gallic style of New Orleans' balconied houses.

Further along the Thames, near Chertsey, there is a row of converted launches owned mostly by young, single people. Here moorage fees are paid to the owners of the land along the river's banks, and very little in the way of shoreside services is provided. The setting is rustic in the Chertsey area, and the feeling one gets there is that the houseboats are truly out in the country. The average launch is 70 to 80 years old, used originally for cargo. Along the bottom inside of the hull is a solid oak beam, called the "kelson," measuring approximately 18 × 18 inches, and running the length of the boat like a wooden spine. The rudder and anchor, each weighing several tons, create downward pressure at both ends of the flexible kelson, causing it to bow upwards in the middle when the hull is empty. Originally, when the boats were used for cargo, the full load of about 50 tons would create the right balance between the kelson and the rudder and anchor at each end of the boat. But today, since the launches are used for living only, the weight in the hold is minimal, and thus the kelson beams tend to bow upwards. As years pass, the bowing will increase, until one day the hull may not withstand the strain of the spine-like kelson beam, but will simply crack in half.

Chertsey houseboat owners are proud of their restoration of these old launches. They enjoy both the work and the play that comes so easily when living on the river. They talk of living a bit closer to nature than most of their landlubber friends—referring not only to the animal- and water-life and natural setting, but also to basic daily chores such as cooking, washing, disposing of waste, and keeping their homes shipshape.

On a nearby stretch of the River Thames, between Hampton Court and Kingston Bridge, houseboats are moored here and there along the banks. It is in this area that the old black boat bearing the motto "Our boats are our homes" can be found amid a small, commune-like cluster of houseboats occupied mostly by young people and their young children. Several small but conventional floating homes are moored at a marina nearby. And on the other bank of the river, moored in solitude, is a unique houseboat with rounded ends, a tile roof, and a lovely columned walkway all around the boat.

In the Thames not far from Hampton Court is a small, almost camouflaged isle called Tagg's Island. It is one of the few places in England used exclusively by modern floating homes in an organized, legally secure, family-oriented community. Tagg's Island has a distinctly suburban atmosphere. The floating homes are new-looking and neatly furnished, with all the conveniences of small private homes on land. Most of the houseboats here have "backyards"; that is, sizeable grassy areas alongside their moorages used for play, picnicking, gardening, etc. Many of these yards are fenced off, again lending the effect of a suburban environment.

The Tagg's Island community, with its stable atmosphere, modern methods of sanitation, approved access to water and other utilities and services, had to organize in order to establish its security. Like those who struggled and succeeded in Seattle, this English island of houseboats now reaps the beauty of its surroundings and the special pleasures that go along with houseboat living.

Several houseboats on the River Thames in central London, located in the Chelsea area, by the Battersea Bridge. *A:* children entering their box-type floating home. *B:* small pontoon boat placed aboard a shallow barge base, here resting on the mud at low tide.

A

B

"Narrow boats" in London's famous "Little Venice," an area of intersecting canals in a charming residential neighborhood. *A:* gaily painted traditional narrow boat with original rudder still intact. *B:* several characteristic houseboats on a quiet and pretty canal. *C:* efficient use of space makes the bedroom of this long, thin boat appear much wider than it really is.

A

B

C

Nearby, on a narrow boat, one can see an excellent example of traditional narrow-boat painting, particularly the castle and flower motifs.

Typical retired launch boat, now fully converted
for living, is moored along the Thames in the area
of Chertsey.

This nicely furnished interior is in a converted cargo boat moored near Chertsey. The illustration clearly shows the powerful kelson beam, the "spine" of the boat, that runs along the inside bottom of the hull.

The lovely *Astoria*, a riverboat-style floating home whose decor is reminiscent of New Orleans French architecture.

Exquisitely restored narrow boat in the Hampton
Court area of the River Thames. *Right:* details of
two of the exterior paintings.

Near Kingston Bridge, on the Thames, is a small
and united community of English houseboat
dwellers.

On another stretch of the Thames, near Hampton Court, is a remarkable two-story, tiled-roof houseboat with a columned walkway all around.

Holland

Nowhere in the world is modern houseboat living so firmly established and so much a part of a city's culture as in Amsterdam. In a city that has almost as many canals as streets, and where in recent decades living space has been both limited and expensive, it follows that a sizeable number of Amsterdammers would turn to the canals as the site of their homes.

Almost all of Amsterdam's houseboats are retired canal and oceangoing barges, falling into two categories — the tjalk, by far the more common, having a round snub-nosed bow and stern rising almost vertically from the water; and the clipper, with a long pointed bow rising at a long graceful angle from the water. Most of these barges were built around the turn of the century and worked as cargo carriers until World War II, when larger, more efficient cargo ships displaced them. Still, some of the present houseboats were eking out a living for cargo-toting families as recently as the late 1960's, as a few still struggle to do today.

It wasn't until the mid-fifties that houseboat living in barges — that is, in the full length of the barge — was even legally possible. The hulls until that time were controlled by Dutch Customs; these cargo areas were locked and the only living space was therefore the small cabin area at the stern of the barge. The government was more liberal with box-type (non-barge) houseboat living, which was permitted just following World War II. These houseboats had no engines, thus could not move around and clog up canal traffic.

Today there are several thousand houseboats lining the canals of Amsterdam. The water authority's main concern is the overcrowding that occurs when one boat moors alongside another, tending to block the center of the canal. Nevertheless, the houseboat population in Amsterdam is on the increase. People of all ages and backgrounds inhabit the canals. They treat their houseboats with love and a lighthearted sense of decor, for most of the boats are gaily painted and many abound with plants and flowers. The canals often look like a festival of houseboats.

Some of the houseboats maintain their original shape (much like the péniche in France), with little or no superstructure built above the deep hull. But others have elaborate rooms, studios, play and sunning areas built on top of the long hulls, maximizing the vertical possibilities of living on a barge. There are Amsterdam houseboats that can be called eccentric, such as the 1890-built tjalk belonging to an artist known as "Victor Four," who has used straw for the main external covering. He has also annexed several completely straw-covered rafts to his main boat, creating a rustic, floating-barn effect. The main barge seems to overflow with flowers, plants, sculpture, and fascinating accumulations of found objects.

There are several widely known marijuana houseboats in Amsterdam, boats that grow and sell the living, bright green plants. This horticultural business is quite legal, owing to a Dutch law that does not regard as illicit the selling of living *cannabis* plants, but only the dried leaves, stems, and buds. Thus the "grass" boats grow their plants in full view of the public and,

obviously, the authorities. One of the boats, *The Lowlands Weed Co.*, is listed in the Amsterdam yellow pages under "Hemp Products" — the only entry in that classification. The boat itself is a tjalk, originally used as a sailing cargo ship to transport peat. It was built in 1898 and was worked until 1954, when its last captain retired. The present owner bought it in 1961. He moved aboard with his wife and within a few years had two children, both born on the boat. In 1968 he began to conceive of the boat as a publicity symbol for marijuana, and has since that time succeeded in attracting all of Amsterdam and much of Holland to the "cause" of marijuana. To further attract passersby, he built a large studio-like superstructure above the approximately 65 × 13 foot hull. And on top of the 45-foot mast he built a bench and facing chair, accommodating up to three people who "wish to feel high."

In no other city is there a houseboat for cats alone. Supported by donations from visitors and citizens, *De Amsterdamse Poezenboot*, or catboat, is a famous tourist attraction. Dozens of stray cats have been given a permanent and comfortable home on a canal, right next to other houseboats accommodating people. Nearing the *Poezenboot*, one can usually hear camera shutters clicking away, and the bemused laughter of passersby. A modest, hand-painted sign on the side of the boat tells the story: "*Wy Waren Zwerfpoezen. Uw gift is ons leven*" (We were nomadic cats. Your gift is our life).

But not all Dutch houseboats are eccentric or humorous. Most are simply homes for people who are into the pleasurable business of houseboat living. Many serve also as studios for painters, sculptors, dancers, and writers — people who therefore spend most of their time aboard these roomy barges.

Some of the boats have interesting histories, such as the *Verwisseling*, a traditional Dutch name meaning, literally, "changing in function or place," but understood as "always something different." The *Verwisseling*'s hull was built in 1890–93. The rest of the boat was completed and enlarged in 1913, when it began sailing (no engine yet) between Holland and Spain, transporting freight. It was owned by one family and used to move cargo until World War II. An internal-combustion engine was added by the Germans, who during the War intended to use the boat for transporting ammunition. But the owners, like many Dutch owners of motorized cargo boats, sank the vessel before the Germans could put it to use. Still, the occupying army raised the *Verwisseling* from the bottom, repaired it, and used it as an ammo carrier for several years. Then it was abandoned. The present owner has had the boat, and lived on it, since 1965.

Although the densest concentration of Dutch houseboats is in Amsterdam there are many hundreds more in various other regions of this flat country, which has intricate systems of canals throughout. In some of the outlying areas of Amsterdam, one can find a wide assortment of houseboats — both in communities and in rustic isolation. In the former category is the houseboat village of Ijsbaanpad, south of Amsterdam's city center. Here in a quiet suburban setting is a huge group, perhaps 200 to 250, of floating homes. Most of these houseboats float on pontoons or shallow barge bases. The superstructures are almost all box-type houses, most with flat roofs, but some with conventional slanted roofs. Most of the residents at Ijsbaanpad are middle-income working people and their families. The floating homes are tightly clustered, with approximately four-foot docks between the dozens of rows at the moorage site. Except for one or two unusually designed houseboats, most look like typical suburban land houses moved from front lawns to pontoon bases.

In a quaint country village farther outside Amsterdam, Rijnwaterwoude, there is a single houseboat occupied by a retired Dutch businessman and his wife. The boat, a small tjalk, 65 × 14 feet, was built as a sailing cargo ship in 1904. Named *Twee Gebroeders* (Two Brothers), it was worked until 1952, when it was converted for living. The present owners have used it since 1959, proudly describing how their family of several children "practically grew up on it." This beautifully designed blue-and-white houseboat is made of high-quality oak wood, shaped in a long, graceful curve from bow to stern of the hull. The window frames, too, are slightly curved in harmony with the rest of the structure. The interior is as charming as the exterior, with a full-sized kitchen, dining area, and sitting room. Several cozy bedrooms are located deeper in the hold, with enough small sleeping nooks to accommodate eight people comfortably.

The houseboats of Holland are among the most beautiful and varied anywhere. It is not just the boats themselves, however, that attract the eye and invite the praise of observers. It is the spirit and warmth of the people living aboard them, so easily evidenced as one strolls along the numerous canals, taking in the bright colors, sparkling-clean windows, dozens of floral clusters, pets, children, and an endless variety of decorative art and artifacts.

A

A: characteristically colorful tjalk moored in
central Amsterdam. Note the blunt, rounded bow.
B: long, graceful bow identifies this as a
clipper-type houseboat. *C:* main sitting room of
the clipper, with bedspread used as ceiling
decoration.

C

B

View over a tjalk's stern of a boxy houseboat on the opposite bank. The building beyond is typical Dutch architecture, including one of the many gold-lettered chiming clocks seen in Amsterdam.

Stately and well-maintained tjalk houseboat on the Prinsengracht canal. One can see several other kinds of houseboats on the opposite bank.

An almost modernistic all-wood superstructure is built onto this tjalk hull. An extra room actually extends over the water beyond the stern. Behind the houseboat is a traditional Amsterdam warehouse.

Box-type houseboats on Prinseneiland, near Amsterdam's central train station. Here, a train speeds by the moored boats.

A

B

A: detail of an artist's houseboat showing humorous carved figures. *B:* charming "patio" area in front of the houseboat *Anna* on one of Amsterdam's prettiest canals, the Prinsengracht.

Stylishly designed interior sitting room on tjalk owned by a Dutch artist.

A houseboat on the Amsteldijk, one of many in Holland that seemingly overflow with plants and flowers.

Left: Artist " Victor Four's" tjalk houseboat behind his two straw-covered raft-barges used as extra rooms and studio space. *Right:* The gangway connecting the raft-barges (the port side of the main boat is at right).

The Lowlands Weed Company, one of several boats in Holland growing and selling the live *cannabis* plant. *A:* full view of the tjalk with its unique superstructure. The rear "mast" is actually an old tree held up by cables. *B:* main sitting room of the marijuana boat, designed and executed by the owner, whose two children were born on the houseboat. *C:* detail of upper portions of superstructure, showing the bench and seat atop the main mast.

B

A

C

Two details of another "weed" boat, this one called *Micky Grass*. *A:* the entrance is a Disneyesque mouth whose front teeth are the main doors. *B:* bow of the tjalk-type boat, overflowing with bright green marijuana plants.

A

B

On the canal known as the Singel one can see a popular Amsterdam tourist attraction, the *Poezenboot,* or catboat—probably the only houseboat in the world given to stray cats as their permanent home.

A unique boat in the Ijsbaanpad community, featuring several decks with beautiful, curved windows.

Outside central Amsterdam, in an area called
Ijsbaanpad, there is a middle-income community
of several hundred houseboats moored closely
together in an inlet. We see two typical box-type
houseboats, one on a pontoon base, the other on a
tjalk hull.

Detail of houseboat in background of photo at
left. Above the richly lacquered front door is a flat
log railing that runs around the entire upper deck
of this floating home.

Surely one of the quaintest boats in Holland, this gracefully designed and prettily painted tjalk, called *Twee Gebroeders* (Two Brothers), was built in 1904. *A:* the starboard side, showing the superstructure's gently curved line that conforms to the curve of the hull. *B:* interior, showing one of the small rooms in the original hull, with stained-glass window on door, working fireplace with traditional Dutch tiles, and small sleeping compartment at right.

A

B

On a canal in the country town of Purmerend, one
can see this cheerful houseboat, particularly
noteworthy for its charmingly designed pigeon
coop atop the main superstructure.

In a splendid rural setting, on a canal called
Ringvaart, near the town of Sloten, is this dark,
almost brooding, houseboat built on a tjalk base.
Such isolated houseboats are a familiar sight as
one drives around the scenic, flat, canal-filled
countryside of Holland.

Turkey and Italy

It is odd that two countries so famous for their rivers and seas have virtually no houseboats on their waters. Several authoritative sources in the U.S. indicated that houseboats could be found in both Istanbul and Rome. Yet once there, it was apparent that few if any exist, not only in these cities but in other parts of either country.

In central Istanbul, with its scenic and historical Bosphorus, separating the Sea of Marmara in the south from the Black Sea in the north, the one boat "lived on" is a huge, all-metal utility boat. Located at the foot of the Ataturk Bridge, it serves as an office for the Istanbul Port Authority. When not on duty, certain officers who work on the boat spend their nights there; that is, they sleep in. It is clearly not a *houseboat*.

At Kumkapi, on the southern shore of central Istanbul, is a commercial boat basin with many large-sized fishing and cargo boats on the main docks. Behind the docks there is a narrow, shallow inlet used for mooring about 35 small fishing dinghies. Amid these is an old, half-sunken (retired) fishing boat with a tin-roofed structure on top. It is used only on special occasions. When sudden heavy storms come up, fishermen race in from the bay and put up for the night in this decrepit, but still useful, vessel. Across the inlet at Kumkapi, behind the small dinghies, is a semi-houseboat—"semi," in that half the structure rests on a narrow dock behind it, while the other half either rests on the mud, or, at high tide, floats on metal drums. It is sparsely furnished by the crusty caretaker of the dinghies, who uses his shack as an overnight place when he does not return to his regular home on land.

North of Istanbul is the lovely resort area of Tarabya. (The English word "therapy" is derived from Tarabya. From the fifth to seventh centuries B.C., pregnant women traveled to Tarabya to drink a special spring water thought to "cure" them—make them healthy during their pregnancy and guarantee strong, normal babies. It was also thought that bathing in the choppy waters coming in from the Black Sea was another "cure" for pregnant women.) At a small marina in one of Tarabya's resort bays, there are two "boxes" on flat, floating bases, each box perhaps 10 × 10 feet. These one-room, newly built structures are actually floating cabañas, not houseboats. They are used in summer by children of the rich to swim from, change clothing, and sometimes sleep in.

Why doesn't Turkey have houseboats? The people do not consider them safe to live in. There is fear of storms and swift currents. Where others in the world welcome the sensation of floating, of constant movement, the Turks consider living on water to be unstable, impermanent. A source in Turkey, asked for his explanation, summed it up tersely: "Modern Turks are too bourgeois for houseboats."

Sources in New York had advised that houseboats could be found in many parts of Italy—even in the heart of Rome, on a small island, Isola Tiberina, in the Tiber River.

Isola Tiberina, as it turns out, has not one houseboat around it. It is entirely possible that it never has, since this tiny isle in a narrow part of the river has no capacity to moor boats safely in the relatively fast Tiber River currents. Isola Tiberina has a few private dwellings built on one end of it; most of the islet is occupied by a health clinic.

Exploring other parts of the Tiber in Rome, one can find several floating sunbathing clubs, known as *stabilimenti*. Reputedly, one or two of these recreation boats are lived on by the caretakers. Some of the Roman backdrops are compelling, such as the *stabilimenti* sitting at the foot of Castel Sant'Angelo, by the bridge of the same name. The question comes up as to whether or not *stabilimenti* are houseboats. They look like houseboats, but what about their main function?

The Italian term for houseboat is *casa galeggiante*. Every Italian who offers information and advice about houseboats seems to know exactly what the term means, but doesn't know where they are to be found. It's a pity—such a nice name for something that apparently doesn't exist!

A pessimistic policeman explained that while there are surely houseboats in other parts of Italy, "people around the Tiber would not want to live on this river. It is a dead river. The current is slowed down by man-made underwater walls to prevent the decay and erosion of Rome's many bridge columns. Thus, the river is not navigable except for very short distances. In this sense, the river is dead. And who would be silly enough to want to live on a river when one can live normally on land?"

West of Rome, at the coastal resort towns of Ostia and Fiumicino, there are no houseboats to be found, even amid the thousands of sailboats and cruisers at marinas along the inlets leading to the sea.

On the southern tip of Italy's boot, in the harbor of Reggio, and at nearby Messina on Sicily, there again are no houseboats. Indeed, no *case galeggianti* exist in all of Sicily, explained the Sicilian Tourist Agency.

In Northern Italy, just south of Milan, in the area of Pavia, the Ticino River runs southeast for about four miles, to where it meets the Po. Here, along this quiet, scenic river are five or six small, boxy houses on boat hulls or barge bases. Conspicuously quiet and locked up, it turns out that the Ticino houseboats are not lived in, but used recreationally on summer weekends as floating cottages.

On Lake Como, the famous resort area north of Milan, the calm waters—seemingly ideal for houseboat living—unfortunately contain no *case galeggianti*.

With all the water in and around Istanbul, it is remarkable that the closest thing to a houseboat is in this picture. Here, at Kumkapi, is a white-roofed "semi-houseboat," half on a dock and half in the water, used by a caretaker who sleeps there occasionally.

Along the beautiful banks of Rome's Tiber River are a handful of "stabilimenti," houseboat-like structures, used as sunbathing clubs.

Acknowledgments

In a book that occasioned a trip around the world, with the willing cooperation of governments, tourist organizations, houseboat associations, guides, friends, and friends of friends—not to mention the several hundred individuals whose houseboats I boarded—it is plainly impossible to thank each as I would like to do. Space limits me to acknowledging those who were the principal sources of help in the many locations that I (and my gifted photographers) visited: Miami Beach: Todd Gabor, Joe Marks, and Patti Dubin; Fort Lauderdale: Lillian and Bill McComas; New Orleans: Judy Newman; Washington: Natalie Roush and Terry Pettus; California: Beverly Dubin and Andrea Goodman; Hong Kong: Gladis and Gordon DePree, Eddie Sterenberg, Pauline and Bert Israel, Graham Hornel, and Sandra Taylor; Thailand: Mrs. Amara Apichatyotin and Anumat Todayong; Kashmir: Habib Boktoo, his sons Latif and Aslam, and Akber, a special human being; Turkey: Mrs. Guler Kirdar and Oryal Belener; Rome: Dennis Redmont and Ned Teitelbaum; Milan: Andrew Heath; Paris: Xavier Esselinck, Jean-Loup Nitot, and Marie-Paule Bournonville; London: Jon Ison, Jan Pienkowski, and David Walser; Amsterdam: Eddy Posthuma de Boer. Special thanks go to Bill Ullman for his many invaluable introductions in Asia and Europe.

To my friend and mentor, Andreas Landshoff, I extend heartfelt thanks for his total support. And, finally, deepest gratitude to Ted and Caroline Robbins for providing the space, sustenance, warmth, and confidence during the months of work on this book.

M.G.

Photography Credits

John Blaustein — 10, 11, 12 (top), 13, 14, 15, 16, 17, 21 (top), 22 (A), 23 (C, D), 24, 25 (bottom), 26, 27 (top), 28, 29, 50, 51, 52, 53, 54, 55, 56 (A), 64 (bottom), 65 (top), 66 (A), 67, 68, 69, 71, 74, 76 (top), 77, 78 (bottom left), 80, 82 (A, B), 83, 84, 85, 89, 90, 91, 92, 93, 94, 97 (A), 98, 99 (C, bottom), 101, 103, 104, 105, 59 (left)

Mark Gabor — 11 (A), 12 (bottom), 18, 21 (bottom), 22 (B), 25 (top), 27 (bottom), 32, 33 (A), 34 (A, C), 56 (B), 57, 58, 59, 60-1, 64 (top), 65 (bottom), 66 (B), 70, 75, 76 (bottom), 78 (top left, right), 79, 81, 82 (C), 88, 97 (B), 99 (B), 100, 122, 127

Pedar Ness — 33 (B), 34 (B), 35, 36, 37, 38, 39, 40, 43, 44, 45, 46-7

Eddy Posthuma de Boer — 108, 109, 110, 111, 112, 113, 114, 115, 116, 117, 118, 119, 120, 121, 123, 124, 125